RUNELORE

RUNELORE

THE MAGIC, HISTORY, AND HIDDEN CODES OF THE RUNES

EDRED THORSSON

WEISERBOOKS
San Francisco, CA / Newburyport, MA

First published in 1987 by
Red Wheel/Weiser, LLC
With offices at
665 Third Street, Suite 400
San Francisco, CA 94107
www.redwheelweiser.com

ISBN 978-0-87728-667-7

Library of Congress Cataloging-in-Publication Data
Thorsson, Edred
        Runelore : a handbook of esoteric runology.
        Bibliography : p.
        1. Rune—Miscellanea. 2. Magic 3. Inscriptions, Runic.
    4. Old Norse poetry. I. Title.
    BF1623.R89T49   1987
    133.3'3   86-24719

Cover design by Stewart Williams
Cover photo © Niklas Stjerna

Printed in the United States of America

19 18 17 16 15 14 13

Contents

*This book is given
to all those who strive toward the*
RUNES

About the Cover

The Brö stone is an example of a Medieval memorial stone, discussed in Chapter 3. On the surface, its message reads: "Ginnlog, Hölmgel's daughter, sister of Sygröd and of Got, she had this bridge built and raised this stone after Assur her husband, son of Hákon the earl. He was guardian against the Vikings together with Geter. God help now his spirit and soul." As was common with runic memorial stones, it is possible that a deeper occult meaning is encoded into *how* the runes were actually carved. From a historical perspective, this stone gives us a glimpse of the Swedish coastal defense organization that kept watch against Viking raiders. The Brö stone probably dates to the late 1100's, and is located in Uppsala, the ancient sacred capital of pagan Sweden.

List of Abbreviations

All translations from Old Norse, Old English, and other old languages found in this book are those of the author. An attempt has been made to strike a balance between poetic and literal translations, but often favor is given to the literal for the sake of correct understanding. In such cases notes may be added.

B.C.E.	Before Common Era (= B.C.)
C.E.	Common Era (= A.D.)
Gmc.	Germanic
Go.	Gothic
MS(S)	Manuscript(s)
OE	Old English
OHG	Old High German
ON	Old Norse
pl.	plural
sg.	singular

Transliterations of Old Norse and Germanic Terms

Certain special Germanic graphics have been transliterated in this book. The following are in keeping with certain spelling conventions of the Middle Ages:

ð	dh
þ	th
ǫ	ö

Preface

This book is intended to supplement the practical material found in my *Futhark: A Handbook of Rune Magic* published by Samuel Weiser, Inc. In these pages the more intellectual aspects of the runes—their history and development and their esoteric lore—will be investigated. It is hoped that through this work I can begin to dispel most of the misconceptions fostered by recent books that purport to explore the runic tradition. *Runelore* incorporates into a system of living philosophy and practice the latest and best scientific scholarship of runologists from all over the world. The method used in the present book is essentially one of intuition firmly based on hard scientific data. This is a method that I hope will continue to find wide acceptance. As it stands, *Runelore* is the basic textbook for members of the Rune-Gild, but I trust it will strike a responsive cord in all who seek to unravel the riddle of the runes.

Those interested in continuing runic research are invited to write to

The Rune-Gild
P.O. Box 7622
Austin, TX 78713
USA

Acknowledgments

Thanks go to Mitchell Edwin Wade, David Bragwin James, Robert Zoller, Alice Rhoades, Anthony Looker, Adolf and Sigrun Schleipfer, and Michael A. Aquino.

Introduction

Long have we dwelt outside the gates of the gard of our indwelling gods. We were not expelled from their knowledge by some irreversible transgression—but rather have only turned our backs on their troth. We can again turn to face their radiant power—but only by knowing the roadways of that journey. Those gangways are the runes—the mysteries of our path—and the keys to their own hidden dimensions.

In an elder age we made a mistake. We rejected—slowly and incompletely to be sure, but nevertheless, we as a people rejected—the wisdom of the gods. No wondrous "cure" will reverse this rejection overnight, no "grace" is forthcoming from Ódhinn! Only our own hard efforts will bring each of us back to the long-lost lore. To this difficult yet noble task, all of the efforts of this book and of the Rune-Gild are dedicated.

Although we lost much through our mistakes in ancient times, we have continued to lose in more recent years by misguided efforts of limited vision at the "revival" of the old ways of the North. Again and again, would-be revivalists have rejected the timelessly eternal and positive vision of the Master of Ecstasy in favor of historical, limited schemes of negative ideologies. One of our most important works is to help shape a philosophical foundation for the growth of this positive vision of timeless relevance, that we may win by example and conquer the world from within our Selves.

The runes, and the ideology they encompass, serve a wide variety of ends, through both "direct," or magical, means and more intellectual pathways. In the magical realms, runework is used for personal transformation, building wider consciousness, psychic development, healing, investigation of Wyrd, and shaping the environment according to the inner will.

While in the intellectual realms—to which this book is dedicated—runelore and rune wisdom can serve as a mental framework for the development of a new philosophy based on a timeless pattern and expressed through a potent meta-language. Many "traditions" have tried and failed to construct such a successful meta-language, with a precise and meaningfully beautiful grammar—for example, Judaism, Christianity, Islam and all of their cultural variants. But each may be called a failure because of the inherent weakness in their inorganic systems. If you work through the runic system and make it a part of your life, you will have given yourself a gift no one else could have bestowed: knowledge of *thine own self*—unique yet part of a whole. The runes will serve as a language with which you may "converse" with aspects of yourself and at the same time *communicate* this knowledge to others, which is a hard yet necessary test for any true understanding.

Not only must we understand the runes as the ancients understood them—that is only the beginning—but we must come to a *new knowledge* of them. As they have transformed us, so must our comprehension of them be transformed. They were, are, and shall ever be eternally changing and eternally demanding of change. Therefore, those who wish only to reinforce their personal prejudices and who have little interest in, or indeed fear of, the transmuting powers housed in the runes should be warned now. The runes describe a road of metamorphosis, not a tower of justification.

Like all things *worth* knowing, these mysteries are stubborn secrets (and mischievousness is not beyond them). Often they will wrap themselves in a riddle, but they will always tell more by their riddle than if they had spoken with a clear tongue. There is little grace in their characters, and their Master has even less. But this is as it *must* be. Anyone who says differently must indeed be a priest of the lie—for he would tell you that the *only* gain is by the gift, whereas we Odians know well that true wisdom must be won by the human will. This will and its attendant human consciousness is the only true Gift—it is the sword cast before infant humanity in the cradle. It is by this sword alone that our ways in the world shall be won.

This book is designed to facilitate an effective use of the shaping and imaginative intellect in conjunction with the most recent and best scholarship in the fields of runic studies and in the history of the old Germanic religion. It contains a detailed historical account of the development of ancient runic traditions and the ways in which runestaves were used in the elder age. These historical data are combined with esoteric investigations into the nature of the runes themselves—the ways in which they relate to one another—and into the realms of esoteric teachings of cosmogony, cosmology, numerology, psychology (soul-lore), and theology. This volume provides the details of much that was only hinted at in the pages of *Futhark*. It is hoped that the deeper runelore held in the pages of this work will open the way to a broader understanding of the runes and help to awaken that great god that lies sleeping within. Now its voice may be but a whisper, but with will and craft we shall awaken it, so that its voice becomes a roar—and we will know it more truly than ever before.

Part One

Historical Lore

The Elder Runes
(to 800 C.E.)

This chapter is intended to provide the runester with a basic outline of runic history and development from the oldest times to around 800 C.E. (or the beginning of the Viking Age) and includes a section on the Old English and Frisian traditions that continue beyond that time frame. It is necessary for anyone entering upon the esoteric study of the runes to have a fundamental notion of the historical context of the tradition. *Runelore* will provide the foundation for this task; independent readings and studies must build the larger edifice. The majority of the information contained in this first part of the book has been gleaned from scholarly works on runology (see Bibliography). The exoteric facts and interpretations contained in these pages will serve the runester well as an introduction to the wondrous world of rune wisdom developed in the second half of the book.

The Word *Rune*

The most common definition for the word *rune* is "one of the letters of an alphabet used by ancient Germanic peoples." This definition is the result of a long historical development, the entirety of which we must come to know before we can see how incomplete such a definition is. Actually, these "letters" are much more than signs used to represent the sounds of a language. They are in fact actual *mysteries*, the actual "secrets of the universe," as one will learn who studies them long and hard enough.

Rune as a word is only found in the Germanic and Celtic languages. Its etymology is somewhat uncertain. There are, however, two possible etymologies: (1) from Proto-Indo-European *reu-* (to roar and to whisper), which would connect it with the vocal performance of magical incantations, and (2) from Proto-Indo-European *gwor-w-on-*, which would connect it to the Greek and Old Indic gods *Ouranos* and *Varuna*, respectively, giving the meaning of "magical binding." This is also an attribute of Ódhinn. The word may have had the essential meaning of "mystery" from the beginning.

In any case, a Germanic and Celtic root *runo-* can be established, from which it developed in the various Germanic dialects. That the word is very archaic in its technical sense is clear from its universal attribution with a rich meaning. The root is found in every major Germanic dialect (see table 1.1). What is made clear from the evidence of this table is that "rune" is an ancient, indigenous term and that the oldest meaning was in the realm of the abstract concept (mystery), *not* as a concrete sign (letter). The definition "letter" is strictly secondary, and the primary meaning must be "mystery."

This root is also found in the Celtic languages, where we find Old Irish *rūn* (mystery or secret) and Middle Welsh *rhin* (mystery). Some people have argued that the root was borrowed from Celtic into Germanic; however, more have argued the reverse because the Germanic usages are more vigorous and widespread and richer in meaning. Another possibility is that it is a root shared by the two Indo-European dialects and that there is no real

Table 1.1. Germanic Rune Definition

Dialect	Word	Meaning
Old Norse	*rún*	secret, secret lore, wisdom; magical signs; written characters
Gothic	*rūna*	secret, mysterium
Old English	*rûn*	mystery, secret council
Old Saxon	*rūna*	mystery, secret
Old High German	*rūna*	mystery, secret

question of borrowing in the strict sense. Perhaps the term also was borrowed into Finnish from Germanic in the form *runo* (a song, a canto of the *Kalevala*), but the Finnish word may actually come from another Germanic word meaning "row" or "series."

Although the word is clearly of common Germanic stock, the actual word as we have it in modern English is not a direct descendant from the Old English *rūn* but was borrowed from late scholarly (seventeenth-century) Latin—*runa* (adjective, *runicus*)—which in turn was borrowed from the Scandinavian languages.

The Odian definition of rune is complex and is based on the oldest underlying meaning of the word—a mystery, archetypal secret lore. These are the impersonal patterns that underlie the substance/nonsubstance of the multiverse and that constitute its being/nonbeing. Each of these runes also may be analyzed on at least three levels:

- Form (ideograph and phonetic value)
- Idea (symbolic content)
- Number (dynamic nature, revealing relationships to the other runes)

For a more detailed exploration of the content of the runes see chapter 9. With the runes, as with their Teacher, Ódhinn, all things may be identified—and may be negated. Therefore, any definition that makes use of "profane" language must remain inadequate and incomplete.

Throughout this book, when the word *rune* is used, it should be considered in this complex light; whereas the terms *runestave*, or simple *stave*, will be used in discussions of them as letters or signs.

Early Runic History

The systematic use of runestaves dates from at least 50 C.E. (the approximate date of the Meldorf brooch) to the present. However, the underlying traditional and hidden framework on which the system was constructed cannot be discussed in purely historical terms—it is ahistorical.

Essentially, the history of the runic system spans four epochs: (1) the elder period, from the first century C.E. to about 800 C.E.; (2) the younger period, which takes us to about 1100 (these two periods are expressions of unified runic traditions bound in a coherent symbology); (3) the middle period, which is long and disparate and which witnessed the decay of the external tradition and its submersion into the unconscious; and finally, (4) the periods of rebirth. Although the use of runes continued in an unbroken (but badly damaged) tradition in remote areas of Scandinavia, most of the deep-level runework took place in revivalist schools after about 1600.

It may be argued that a historical study is actually unnecessary or even detrimental for those who wish to plumb the depths of that timeless, ahistorical, archetypal reality of the runes themselves. But such an argument would have its drawbacks. Accurate historical knowledge is necessary because conscious tools are needed for the rebirth of the runes from the unconscious realms; the modern runic investigator must know the origins of the various structures that come into contact with the conscious mind. Only in this context can the rebirth occur in a fertile field of growth. Without the roots the branches will wither and die. For all of this to take place, the runester must have a firm grasp on the history of the runic tradition. In addition, the analytical observation and rational interpretation of objective data (in this case the historical runic tradition) is fundamental to the development of the whole runemaster and vitki.

RUNIC ORIGINS

As the runes are ahistorical, so also must they be without ultimate origin—they are timeless. When we speak of runic origins, we are more narrowly concerned with the origins of the traditions of the futhark stave system. The questions of archetypal runic origins will be taken up in detail in chapter 10. The runes may indeed be said to have passed through many doors on the way to our perceptions of them and to have undergone many "points of origin" in the worlds.

There are several theories on the historical origins of the futhark system and its use as a writing system for the Germanic dialects. These are essentially four in number: the Latin theory, the Greek theory, the North-Italic (or Etruscan) theory, and the indigenous theory. Various scholars over the years have subscribed to one or the other of these theories; more recently a reasonable synthesis has been approached, but it is still an area of academic controversy.

The Latin or Roman theory was first stated scientifically by L. F. A. Wimmer in 1874. Those who adhere to this hypothesis generally believe that as the Germanic peoples came into closer contact with Roman culture (beginning as early as the second century B.C.E. with the invasion of the Cimbri and Teutones from Jutland), along the Danube (at Carnuntum) and the Rhine (at Cologne, Trier, etc.), the Roman alphabet was adapted and put to use by the Germans. Trade routes would have been the means by which the system quickly spread from the southern region to Scandinavia and from there to the east. This latter step is necessary because the oldest evidence for the futhark is not found near the Roman limes and spheres of influence but rather in the distant northern and eastern reaches of Germania. The idea of trade routes poses no real problem to this theory because such routes were well established from even more remote times. The Mycenaean tombs in present-day Greece (ca. 1400–1150 B.C.E.) contain amber from the Baltic and from Jutland, for example. More recently, Erik Moltke has theorized that the futhark originated in the Danish region and was based on the Roman alphabet.

This theory still holds a number of adherents, and some aspects of it, which we will discuss later, show signs of future importance. In any case, the influence of the cultural elements brought to the borderlands of the Germanic peoples by the Romans cannot be discounted in any question of influence during the period between approximately 200 B.C.E. and 400 C.E.

It must be kept in mind when discussing these theories that we are restricted to questions of the origin of the *idea of writing with a phonetic system* (alphabet) among the Germanic peoples in connection with the runic tradition, and not with the genesis of the underlying system or tradition itself.

The Greek theory, first put forward by Sophus Bugge in 1899, looks more to the east for the origins of this writing system. In this hypothesis it is thought that the Goths adapted a version of the Greek cursive script during a period of contact with Hellenic culture along the Black Sea, from where it was transmitted back to the Scandinavian homeland of the Goths. There is, however, a major problem with this theory because the period of Gothic–Greek contact in question could not have started before about 200 C.E., and the oldest runic inscriptions date from well before that time. For this reason most scholars have long since abandoned this hypothesis. The only way to save it is to prove a much earlier, as yet undocumented connection between the two cultures in question. More research needs to be done in this area. Also, it is probable that Hellenistic ideas, even if they played no role in runic origins, may have had a significant part in the formation of some elements of the traditional system.

The North-Italic or Etruscan theory is perhaps the most interesting, and it is the one that has attracted most scholars in recent years. This idea was first proposed by C. J. S. Marstrander in 1928 and was subsequently modified and furthered by Wolfgang Krause, among others, in 1937. Historically, this hypothesis supposes that Germanic peoples living in the Alps adopted the North-Italic script at a relatively early date—perhaps as early as 300 b.c.e.—when the Cimbri came into contact with it and passed in on to the powerful Suevi (or Suebi), from whom it quickly spread up the Rhine and along the coast of the North Sea to Jutland and beyond. There can be no historical objections to the plausibility of this scenario, except for the fact that the initial contact came some three to four hundred years *before* we have any record of actual runic inscriptions.

As a matter of fact, there is an example of Germanic language written in the North-Italic alphabet—the famous helmet of Negau (from ca. 300 b.c.e.). The inscription may be read from right to left in figure 1.1.

The inscription may be read in words *Harigasti teiwai* . . . and translated "to the god Harigast (= Ódhinn)," or "Harigastiz [and] Teiwaz!" In any case the root meanings of the first two words of the inscription are clear. Hari-gastiz (the guest of the army) and Teiwaz (the god Týr). In later times, it would be normal to expect Ódhinn to be identified by a nickname of this type, and we may well have an early example of it here. Also, this would be an early proof of the ancient pairing of the two Germanic sovereign deities (see chapter 13).

As can be seen from the Negau inscription, the scripts in question bear many close formal correspondences to the runestaves; however, some phonetic values would have to have been transferred. No one Etruscan alphabet forms a clear model for the entire futhark. An unfortunate footnote

Figure 1.1. Inscription on the helm of Negau

to runic history has recently been added by a certain occult writer who in two books has represented a version of the Etruscan script as "the runic alphabet." This has perhaps led to some confusion among those attempting to unravel runic mysteries.

The idea that the runes are a purely indigenous Germanic script originated in the late nineteenth century and gained great popularity in National Socialist Germany. This theory states that the runes are a primordial Germanic invention and that they are even the basis for the Phoenician and Greek alphabets. This hypothesis cannot be substantiated because the oldest runic inscriptions date from the first century C.E. and the oldest Phoenician ones date from the thirteenth and twelfth centuries B.C.E. When this theory was first expounded by R. M. Meyer in 1896, the runes were seen as an originally ideographic (the misnomer used was "hieroglyphic") system of *writing* that then developed into an alphabetic system acrophonetically (i.e., based on the first sound of the names attached to the ideograph). One aspect of this is probably correct: the Germanic peoples seem to have had an ideographic system, but it does not appear to have been used as a writing system, and it is here that the indigenous theory goes astray. It is possible that the ideographic system influenced the choice of runestave shapes and sound values.

From the available physical evidence it is most reasonable to conclude that the runestave system is the result of a complex development in which both indigenous ideographs and symbol systems and the alphabetic writing systems of the Mediterranean played significant roles. The ideographs were probably the forerunners of the runestaves (hence the unique rune names), and the prototype of the *runic system* (order, number, etc.) is probably also to be found in some native magical symbology (see chapter 9).

One piece of possible evidence we have for the existence of a pre-runic symbol system is the report of Tacitus in chapter 10 of his *Germania* (ca. 98 C.E.), where he mentions certain *notae* (signs) carved on strips of wood in the divinatory rites of the Germans. Although the recent discovery of the Meldorf brooch has pushed back the date of the oldest runic inscription to a time before Tacitus wrote the *Germania*, these still could have been some symbol system other than the futhark proper. In any case, it is fairly certain that the idea of using such things as a writing system, as well as the influence governing the choice of certain signs to represent specific sounds, was an influence from the southern cultures.

This summarizes the story with regard to the *exoteric* sciences. But what more can be said about the *esoteric* aspects of runic origins? The runes themselves, as has been said, are without beginning or end; they are eternal patterns in the substance of the multiverse and are omnipresent in all of the worlds. But we can speak of the origin of the runes in human consciousness (and as a matter of fact this is the only point at which we can begin to speak about the "origins" of anything).

For this we turn to the *Elder* or *Poetic Edda* and to the holy rune song of the "Hávamál," stanzas 138 to 165, the so called "Rúnatals tháttr Ódhins" (see also chapter 8). There, Ódhinn recounts that he hung for nine nights on the World Tree, Yggdrasill, in a form of self-sacrifice. This constitutes the runic initiation of the god Ódhinn; he approaches and sinks into the realm of death in which he receives the secrets, the mysteries of the multiverse—the runes themselves—in a flash of inspiration. He is then able to return from that realm, and now it is his function to teach the runes to certain of his followers in order to bring wider consciousness, wisdom, magic, poetry, and inspiration to the world of Midhgardhr—and to all of the worlds. This is the central work of Ódhinn, the Master of Inspiration.

The etymology of the name Ódhinn gives us the key to this "spiritual" meaning. *Ódhinn* is derived from Proto-Germanic *Wōdh-an-az*. *Wōdh-* is inspired numinous activity or enthusiasm; the *-an-* infix indicates the one who is master or ruler of something. The *-az* is simply a grammatical ending. The name is also something interpreted as a pure deification of the spiritual principle of *wōdh*. See chapter 13 for more details of Ódhinic theology.

The figure of Ódhinn, like those of the runestaves, stands at the inner door of our conscious/unconscious borderland. Ódhinn is the communicator to the conscious of the contents of the unconscious and supraconscious, and he/it fills the "space" of all of these faculties. We, as humans, are conscious beings but have a deep need for communication and illumination from the hidden sides of the worlds and ourselves. Ódhinn is the archetype of this deepest aspect of humanity, that which bridges the worlds together in a web-work of mysteries—the runes.

Therefore, in an esoteric sense the runes originate in human conscious-ness through the archetype of the all-encompassing (whole) god hidden deeply in all his folk. For us the runes are born simultaneously with consciousness. But it must be remembered that the runes themselves are beyond his (and therefore our) total command. Ódhinn can be destroyed, but because of his *conscious* assumption of the basic patterns of the runic mysteries (in the Yggdrasill initiation) the "destruction" becomes the road to transformation and rebirth.

Age of the Elder Futhark

As mentioned before, the oldest runic inscription yet found is that of the Meldorf brooch (from the west coast of Jutland), which dates from the middle of the first century C.E. From this point on, the runes form a continuous tradition that is to last more than a thousand years, with one major formal transformation coming at approximately midpoint in the history of the great tradition This is the development of the Younger Futhark from the Elder, beginning as early as the seventh century. But the elder system held on in some conservative enclaves, and its echoes continued to be heard until around 800 C.E. and in hidden traditions beyond that time.

The elder system consists of twenty-four staves arranged in a very specific order (see Table 1 in the Appendix). The only major variations in this order apparently were also a part of the system itself. The thirteenth and fourteenth staves : ᛇ : and : ᛈ : sometimes alternated position; as did the twenty-third and twenty-fourth staves :ᛞ : and : ᛟ :. It should be noted that both of these alternations come at the exact *middle* and *end* of the row.

By the year 250 C.E., inscriptions are already found over all of the territories occupied by the Germanic peoples. This indicates that the spread was systematic throughout hundreds of sociopolitical groups (clans, kindreds, tribes, etc.) and that it probably took place along preexisting networks of cultic traditions. Only about three hundred inscriptions in the Elder Futhark survive. This surely represents only a tiny fraction of the total number of inscriptions executed during this ancient period. The vast majority in perishable materials, such as wood and bone—the most popular materials for the runemaster's craft—have long since decayed. Most of the oldest inscriptions are in metal, and some are quite elaborate and developed.

In the earliest times runestaves were generally carved on mobile objects. For this reason the distribution of the locations where inscriptions have been found tells us little about where they actually were carved. A good illustration of this problem is provided by the bog finds (mostly from around 200 C.E.) on the eastern shore of Jutland and from the Danish archipelago. The objects on which the runes were scratched were sacrificed by the local populace after they had defeated invaders from farther east. It was the invaders who had carved these runes somewhere in present-day Sweden, not the inhabitants of the land where the objects were found. As the situation stands, it seems that before about 200 C.E. the runes were known only in the regions of the modern areas of Denmark, Schleswig-Holstein, southern

Sweden (perhaps also on the islands of Öland and Gotland), and southeastern Norway. As the North Germanic and East Germanic peoples spread eastward and southward, they took the runes with them, so that scattered inscriptions have been found in present-day Poland, Russia, Rumania, Hungary, and Yugoslavia. The runic tradition remained continuous in Scandinavia until the end of the Middle Ages. One of the most remarkable Scandinavian traditions was that of the bracteates, carved between 450 and 550 c.e. in Denmark and southern Sweden (see figure 1.6 on page 16). Two other distinct yet organically related traditions are represented by the Anglo-Frisian runes (used in England and Frisia from ca. 450 to 1100 c.e.) and the South Germanic runes (virtually identical to the North Germanic futhark) used in central and southern Germany (some finds in modern Switzerland and Austria) from approximately 550 to 750 c.e.

Futhark Inscriptions

We have seven examples of inscriptions that represent the futhark row, completely or in fragments, from the elder period. They appear in chronological order in figure 1.2.

The Kylver stone (which was part of the *inside* of a grave chamber), combined with later evidence from manuscript runes, shows that the original order of the final two staves was D–O and that the Grumpan and Vadstena bracteates (which are thin disks of gold stamped with symbolic pictographs and used as amulets) were very commonly fashioned with runes as part of their designs. The Kylver stone has, however, reversed the thirteenth and fourteenth staves to read P–EI instead of the usual EI–P order. The Beuchte brooch contains only the first five runes scratched into its reverse side in the futhark order, followed by two ideographic runes—: ᛉ : *elhaz* and : ᛃ : *jera*—for protection and good fortune. On the column of Breza (part of a ruined Byzantine church and probably carved by a Goth) we find a futhark fragmet broken off after the L-stave and with the B-stave left out. The Charnay brooch also presents a fragment, but it seems intentional for magical purposes. The brooch of Aquincum bears the first *ætt* for the futhark complete. (For discussions of the various aspects of the *ætt* system, see chapters 7 and 9.)

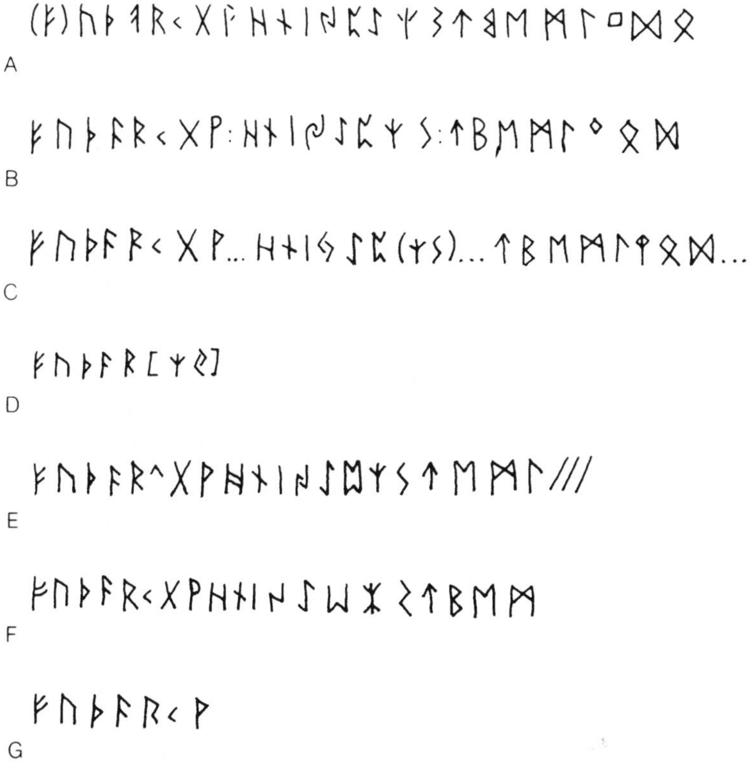

A (ᚹ)ᚺᛒ ᚨᚱ< ᚷ ᚠ ᚺᛏ ᛁ ᛦ ᛈᛋ ᛦ ᛉ ᛏ ᛇᛗ ᛗ ᛚ ᛜᛋᚲ

B ᚠᚢᛒᚠᚱ< ᚷᚠ : ᚺᛏ ᛁ ᛦ ᛋᛉ ᛦ ᛋ : ᛏᛒᛗ ᛗᛚ ᛜ ᚲ ᛨ

C ᚠᚢᛒᚠ ᚱ< ᚷ ᚠ ... ᚺᛏ ᛁ ᚦ ᛋᛉ (ᛏᛋ)... ᛏ ᛒ ᛗ ᛗᛚᛦ ᚲ ᛨ ...

D ᚠᚢ ᛒᚠ ᚱ [ᛦ ᚦ]

E ᚠᚢᛒᚠᚱ^ ᚷ ᛈ ᚺᛏ ᛁ ᚦ ᛋ ᛟ ᛦ ᛋ ᛏ ᛗ ᛗᛚ ///

F ᚠᚢᛒᚠᚱ< ᚷᛈ ᚺᛏ ᛁ ᛦ ᛋ ᚥ ᛦ ᛉᛏᛒᛗᛗ

G ᚠᚢ ᛒ ᚠ ᚱ< ᛈ

Figure 1.2. The Elder Futhark Inscriptions: a) The Kylver Stone, ca. 400; b) The Vadstena/Motala bracteates, ca. 450–550; c) The Grumpan bracteate, ca. 450–550; d) The Beuchte fibula, ca. 450–550; e) The marble column of Breza, ca. 550; f) The Charnay fibula, ca. 550–600; g) The Aquincum fibula, ca. 550.

Survey of the Elder Continental and Scandinavian Inscriptions

The most convenient way to approach exoteric runic history is based on the study of the various types of materials or objects on which staves are carved seen through a chronological perspective. Generally, there are two types of objects: (1) loose, portable ones (jewelry, weapons, etc), which may have been carved in one place and found hundreds or thousands of miles away; and (2) fixed, immobile objects (stones), which cannot be moved at all, or at least not very far.

MOBILE OBJECTS

Runes are found carved on a wide variety of objects: weapons (swords, spearheads and shafts, shield bosses), brooches (also called *fibulae*), amulets (made of wood, stone, and bone), tools, combs, rings, drinking horns, statuettes, boxes, bracteates, buckles, and various metal fittings originally on leather or wood. Most of these had magical functions.

The runic spearheads belong to one of the oldest magico-religious traditions among the Indo-Europeans, and they are among the oldest known inscriptions. The blade of Øvre-Stabu (Norway) was, until the recent Meldorf find, the oldest dated runic artifact (ca. 150 C.E.). On Gotland, the spearhead of Moos dates from 200 to 250. Farther south and to the east, we find the blades of Kovel, Rozvadov, and Dahmsdorf (all from ca. 250). There is also the blade of Wurmlingen, which is much later (ca. 600).

All but Kovel (plowed up by a farmer) and Wurmlingen were found in cremation graves. The Wurmlingen blade is from an inhumation grave. However, their primary function was not funerary; they probably were clanic treasures of magical import that were burned and/or buried with the chieftain. The magical use of the spear in the warrior cult is well known in the Germanic tradition. Hurling a spear into or over the enemy before a battle

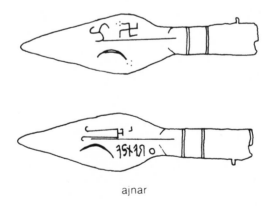

ajnar

Figure 1.3. Spearhead of Dahmsdorf

was a way of "giving" them to Ódhinn, that is, of sacrificing them to the god. Ódhinn himself is said to do this in the primal battle described in the "Völuspá" (st. 24):

> Ódhinn had shot his spear
> over the host

This practice is also known from saga sources.

As an example of these powerful talismanic objects we will examine the blade of Dahmsdorf (found while digging the foundation of a train station in 1865). It is now lost. The blade is made of iron with silver inlay and is probably of Burgundian origin. It is especially interesting because it bears many other symbols besides the runes, as figure 1.3 shows. On the runic side we see a lunar crescent, a *tamga* (a magical sign probably of Sarmatian origin); the nonrunic side shows a triskelion (trifos), a sun-wheel (swastika), and another crescent. The runic inscription reads from right to left: *Ranja*. This is the magical name (in the form of a noun agent) of the spear itself. It is derived from the verb *rinnan* (to run); hence, "the runner." Its function was, in a magical sense, "to run the enemy through" and destroy them.

The brooches, which were used to hold together the cloaks or outer garments of both men and women, were in use from very ancient times (see *Germania*, chapter 17). As such, they were very personal items and ideal for transformation into talismans through the runemaster's craft. And indeed it seems that the majority of the twelve major inscriptions in this class (dating from the end of the second century to the sixth) have an expressly magical function. In six cases this includes a "runemaster formula" in which a special magical name for the runemaster is used. The magical function is either as a bringer of good fortune (active) or as a passive amulet for protection.

For an example of this type of inscription we might look at the brooch of Værløse, which was found in a woman's inhumation grave in 1944. This gilded silver rosette fibula dates from about 200 C.E. The symbology of the object also includes a sun-wheel, which was part of the original design, whereas the runes were probably carved later; at least we can tell that they were carved with a different technique. The inscription can be read in figure 1.4.

Figure 1.4. Værløse inscription

4.   21.   2.   7.   24.   23.

Figure 1.5. Numerical analysis of the Værløse formula

The Værløse runes are difficult to interpret linguistically. Perhaps it is an otherwise unknown magical formula made up of the well-known *alu* (magical power, inspiration; which can be understood in a protective sense), plus *god* (good). The meaning could therefore be "well-being through magical power." It also could be a two-word formula; for example, "*alu* [is wished by] God (agaz)," with the last word being a personal name making use of an ideograph to complete the name. However, the magical formulaic dynamism contained in its numerical value is clear, as we see in figure 1.5.

The numerology of the Værløse formula is a prime example of how numbers of power might have been worked into runic inscriptions. Here we see a ninefold increase of the multiversal power of the number nine working in the realm of six. See chapter 11 for more details on runic numerology.

The bracteates were certainly talismanic in function. Well over 800 of them are known, of which approximately 130 have runic inscriptions. These were not *carved* but rather *stamped* into the thin gold disks with the rest of the design, most commonly an adaptation of a Roman coin. The iconography of these Roman coins, which often show the emperor on a horse, was completely reinterpreted in the Germanic territory, where it came to symbolize

Figure 1.6. Runic bracteate of Sievern

r w r ɪ t u

Figure 1.7. Sievern bracteate inscription

either Óðhinn or Baldr. It is quite possible that the bracteates represent religious icons of the Óðhinic cult.

The Bracteate depicted in figure 1.6 comes from a German find near Sievern (a total of eleven bracteates). The iconography of the Sievern bracteate is also interesting. According to Karl Hauck, the curious formation issuing from the mouth of the head is a representation of the "magical breath" and the power of the word possessed by the god Óðhinn. This can also be seen in representations of the god Mithras. The inscription was badly damaged but probably reads as interpreted in figure 1.7. This reading can be understood as *r(unoz) writu* I carve the runes), a typical magical formula for a runemaster to compose.

As an example of a wooden object preserved by this process we might take the yew box of Garbølle (on Zealand, Denmark) found empty in 1947. It is designed like a modern pencil box with a sliding top and dates from around 400 C.E. The inscription can be read in figure 1.8. The runes are generally interpreted *Hagiradaz ī tawide*: "Hagirad ['one skillful in council'] worked [the staves] in [the box]." The five vertical points after the staves indicate that the reader should count five staves back from there to discover the power behind the runes (: ᚠ :).

There is also a whole range of fairly unique objects that are difficult to classify. Many of them are tools and other everyday objects that have been turned into talismans, whereas some, such as the famous horns of Gallehus and the ring of Pietroassa, are interesting works of art.

The ring of Pietroassa (ca. 350–400) makes a suitable example for these unique objects. It is (or was) a gold *neck ring* with a diameter of about 6

h a g i r a d a R i t a w i d e

Figure 1.8. Garbølle formula

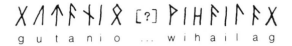

Figure 1.9. Formula of Pietroassa

inches that would be opened and closed with a clasplike mechanism. The ring, along with twenty-two other golden objects (some with jewels), was found in 1837 under a great limestone block by two Rumanian farmers. Unfortunately, almost all of the artifacts have since disappeared or have been heavily damaged. Of the ring only the portion with the inscription itself survives, and that in two pieces. These objects seem to have been the sacred ritual instruments belonging to a pagan Gothic priest-chieftain (perhaps even Athanaric himself?). A neck ring was the insignia of sovereign powers in the pre-Christian Germanic world. Figure 1.9 gives the runic forms as we can now read them. They are to be interpreted as *Gutani* : ᛝ : *wih-hailag*. An unclear sign between runes seven and eight is probably a triskelion, and the eighth rune itself is probably to be read as an ideograph (= *othala*, hereditary property). Therefore, the translation of the whole formula would be something like "The hereditary property of the Goths, sacrosanct."

FIXED OBJECTS

Essentially, there are three types of fixed objects in the elder tradition, all of them in stone but of differing kinds and functions. There are first the rock carvings, cut directly into rock faces, cliffs, and the like. Then there are the so-called *bauta* stones. These stones are specially chosen and dressed and then moved to some predetermined position. The final group is made up of *bauta* stones that also have pictographs carved on them.

Four rock carvings date from between 400 and 550, and all are on the Scandinavian peninsula. They all seem to have a magico-cultic meaning and often refer to the runemaster, even giving hints as to the structure of the Erulian cult.

All of the inscriptions serve as a kind of initiatory declaration of power in which the runemaster carves one or more of his magical nicknames or titles. This type of formula can be used to sanctify an area, to protect it, or even to cause certain specific modifications in the environment.

Figure 1.10. Veblungsnes formula

The simplest example is provided by the rock wall of Veblungsnes in central Norway (see figure 1.10), which dates from about 550. In words, the Veblungsnes formula would read *ek irilaz Wiwila*: "I [am] the Erulian Wiwila." (Note that : ᛗ : is a bind rune combination of : ᛗ : and : < :). The formula consists of the first person pronoun "I," the initiatory title *irilaz* (dialect variation of *erilaz*), the Erulian (widely understood simply as "runemaster"), and the personal name. This name is, however, not the normal given name of the runemaster but a holy or initiatory name. It means "the little sanctified one" or "the little one who sanctifies." It might be pointed out that the name *Wiwilaz* is a diminutive form of *Wiwaz*, which is also found on the stone of Tune, and it is related to the god name Wihaz, (ON Vé). In this formula the runemaster, or Erulian, sanctifies an area by his magical presence. He does this by first *assuming* a divine persona and then *acting* within that persona by carving the runes.

Bauta stones are the forerunners of the great runestones of the Viking Age. Such stones date from between the middle of the fourth century to the end of the seventh, but they continue to develop beyond this time. Inscriptions of this kind are almost always connected with the cult of the dead and funerary rites and/or customs. As is well known, this is an important part of the general Cult of Ódhinn and one with which the runes were always deeply bound. Sometimes the runes were used to protect the dead from would-be grave robbers or sorcerers, sometimes they were employed to keep the dead in their graves (to prevent the dreaded *aptrgöngumenn* ["walking dead"], and sometimes the runes were used to effect a communication with the dead for magical or religious purposes.

The stone of Kalleby, the formula of which can be seen in figure 1.11 on page 20, is an example of the runemaster's craft to cause the dead to stay in their graves, or at least to return to the grave after having wandered abroad for a while. These conceptions are common in many ancient cultures. In the Germanic world, the "undead" were often reanimated by the will of a sorcerer and sent to do his bidding.

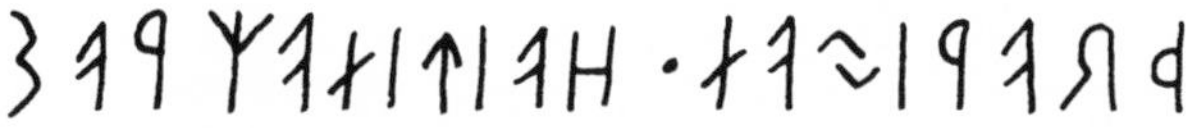

$$ \text{ﾐ卩卩 ﾔ卩ﾄ|介|卩н · ﾄ卩〜|卩卩卩別 d} $$

Figure 1.11. Kalleby formula

The Kalleby formula is to be read from right to left *thrawijan · haitinaz was*: "he [the dead man] was ordered to pine [for the grave]." The use of the past tense is very often found in magical inscriptions for a twofold technical reason: (1) the basic magical dictum "do as if your will *was* already done," and (2) the fact that the ritual that ensured the will of the runemaster had already been performed *before* the actual effect was called upon. These conceptions are fundamental to the Germanic world view concerning the ultimate *reality* of "the past" and its power to control what lies beyond it. The Erulian *uses* this to effect his will.

The pictographic stones combine runic symbology with pictographic magic. This is especially clear in two of the stones, Eggjum and Roes, both of which have schematic representations of horses (see the E-rune). The tradition of combining runestaves and pictographs appears to be very old,

Figure 1.12. Stone of Roes

since the oldest of the four inscription dates from about 450 and the last (Roes) from about 750. The technique would eventually flower into the great pictographic runestone tradition of Viking Age Scandinavia.

Perhaps the best example of the combination of the runes and the horse image is seen on the Gotlandic stone of Roes (see figure 1.12.) This hefty talisman (a sandstone plate 22 by 30 by 3 inches) was found under the roots of a hazel bush during the nineteenth century. The actual runic formula can be read in figure 1.13. Its interpretation is not without controversy, but the best solution seems to be one that makes the complex figure a bind rune of U + D + Z, so that the whole could be read *ju thin Uddz rak*: "Udd drove, or sent this horse out." But what is this supposed to mean?

Old Norse literature provides us with a good clue to the significance of this symbol complex. In *Egil's Saga* (chapter 57) we read how Egil fashioned a *níðhstöng* or cursing pole out of *hazel wood* and affixed a *horse's head* atop it. This pole of insult was intended to drive Erik Blood-Ax and his queen, Gunnhild, out of Norway—and it worked. (See chapter 6 for more details.)

Before leaving the inscriptions of the Elder Futhark it seems proper to say something about the language they employ. It was at about the time that the runestaves began to be used in writing that the Germanic languages really began to break up into distinct dialects. The language of the period before the breakup is called Proto-Germanic (or Germanic). There also seems to have been an early differentiation in the north that can be called Proto-Nordic or Primitive Norse. The Goths who began migrating to the east (into present-day Poland and Russia) from Scandinavia around the beginning of the Common Era developed the East Germanic dialect (which played an important role in the history of the early runic inscriptions). On the Continent to the south a distinctive South Germanic developed that eventually came to include all German, English, and Frisian dialects; whereas in the north

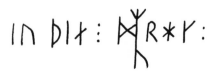

Figure 1.13. Roes formula

Proto-Nordic had evolved into West Norse (in Norway) and East Norse (in Denmark and Sweden). In the first few centuries of the elder period all of these dialects were mutually intelligible; and besides, the runemasters had a tendency to use archaic forms in later inscriptions because they were often ancient and long-standing magical formulas. It has been supposed that there was even a pan-Germanic "sacred" dialect used and maintained by runemasters.

Anglo-Frisian Runes

There are as many reasons for keeping the English and Frisian runic traditions separate as there are for looking at them together. The Frisian tradition is only sparsely known, but it is filled with magical practice; the English is better represented yet less overtly magical in character. However, there are striking similarities in the forms of individual staves, and this fact, coupled with the close cultural ties between the English and Frisians throughout early history, leads us to the conclusion that there was some link in their runic traditions as well. Unfortunately, we have no complete Frisian Futhork.

First let us examine the rich English tradition. The oldest inscription yet found in the British Isles is that on the deer astragalus of Caistor-by-Norwich. It probably dates from the first real wave of Germanic migration during the latter part of the fifth century. But it is perhaps in fact a North Germanic inscription that was either imported or carved by a "Scandinavian" runemaster. This possibility must be considered because the northern form of the H-rune (: ᚼ :) is used and not the English : ᚺ :. The dating and distribution patterns of English runic monuments are difficult because the evidence is so sparse and the objects are for the most part mobile. In all, there are only about sixty English runic artifacts, mostly found in the eastern and southeastern parts of the country before 650 C.E. and mainly in the North Country after that time. The epigraphical tradition (i.e., the practice of *carving* runestaves), which must have begun in earnest as early as 450 C.E., was extinct by the eleventh century. The runestaves found another outlet in the *manuscript* tradition. These are valuable for our study but are rarely magical in nature.

The history of the English runic tradition can be divided into the two periods mentioned above: (1) pre-650 (in which a good deal of heathen ways survive), and (2) 650 to 1100 (which tends to be more Christianized, with less magical or esoteric practice in evidence).

The English Futhorc

The only futhorc inscription that remains to us is on the somewhat faulty Thames scramsax, which dates from around 700 C.E. It is actually a sample of fine Anglo-Saxon metalwork in which the craftsman inlaid silver, copper, and bronze into matrices that had been cut into the iron blade. The order and shape of the runestaves can be seen in Runic Table II (appendix C). This futhorc is followed by a "decorative" pattern, and then comes the personal name Beagnoth—probably that of the swordsmith, not the runemaster. As can be seen, there are a number of what seem to be formal errors as well as ones of ordering. All of this is due, no doubt, to Beagnoth's miscopying of a model. It is fortunate that we have more, if later, evidence that shows that in fact the English runic tradition was both well developed and very close to the Continental one. This evidence comes from the manuscript tradition. The most informative document is, of course, the "Old English Rune Poem" (see chapter 8).

The "Old English Rune Poem" contains a futhorc of twenty-eight staves; the codex Salisbury 140 and the St. John's College MS 17 also record Old English futhorcs of twenty-eight and thirty-three staves, respectively. Another manuscript, the Cottonian Domitian A 9 even records a futhorc divided into *ættir*. Here, it is significant that the *ætt* divisions are made in the same places as those of the Elder Futhark. This demonstrates the enduring nature of the underlying traditions of the Germanic row.

It seems that the oldest runic tradition in England was the Common Germanic row of twenty-four runes, which was quickly *expanded* to twenty-six staves, with a modification of the fourth and twenty-fourth runes: (4) : ᚠ : [a] became : ᚩ : [o]; (24) : ᛟ : had the phonetic value [œ] and later [ē]. In addition, the staveform : ᚨ : was relocated to position 25 and named *æsc* (ash tree). These changes took place as early as the sixth century. As the English language evolved and changed, so did the Old English futhorc. This is the normal way an alphabet develops. As a sound system of a language becomes more complex, so does its writing system.

The use of English runes can be divided into three main classes:

Loose objects

Fixed objects (e.g., stones)

Manuscripts

The loose objects represent the broadest category. They are generally the earliest type of inscription, yet they persist to a late date. Unfortunately, many of them are fragmentary or damaged to such an extent that exact

Figure 1.14. Caistor-by-Norwich inscription

readings are almost impossible. Most of the mobile objects have the runes scratched into metal, bone, or wood; however, some represent the staves by more intricate techniques of metalwork (see the Thames scramsax) or fine wood/bone carving (e.g., the famous Franks Casket). The Old English runestones mostly date from the Christian period and seem to represent a pseudo-Christian adaptation of the tradition, but they may still have magical import. Most of them are actually memorial stones or stone crosses and were carved by skillful stonemasons.

There is no Old English manuscript entirely written in runestaves, but they are nevertheless widely represented in the literature, where they serve both cryptic and pragmatic ends. Two runes were adapted by the English for writing with pen and parchment in the Roman alphabet; they were the Þ < : þ : [th] (*thorn* [thorn]) and the ⱷ < : ⱷ : [w] (*wynn* [joy]). From there this orthographic practice was taken to Germany and to Scandinavia.

The Caistor-by-Norwich inscription mentioned above is a good example of the loose type of object from an early period. Its runes appear in figure 1.14. This bone was found with twenty-nine other similar ones (without runes), along with thirty-three small cylindrical pieces, in a cremation urn. It is possible that the objects were used as lots in divinatory rites. The inscription itself is difficult to interpret, but it may mean "the colorer" or "the scratcher" and be a holy name of the runemaster.

æ   c   o   s   œ   r   i

Figure 1.15. Chessel Down formula

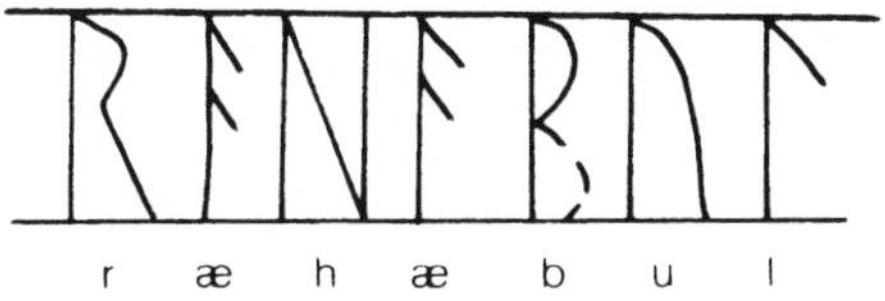

Figure 1.16. Sandwich inscription

An explicit example of magic used by the Odhinic runemasters is hard to come by in the English material, but the scabbard mount of Chessel Down (see figure 1.15) is probably one. The inscription was scratched on the back of the fitting and is thus invisible when in place. It might be translated as "Terrible one, wound [the enemy]!" If this is so, then *æco* (terrible one) would be the name of the sword, and *særi* (wound [!]) its charge.

An interesting example of a magical runestone from the pagan period is provided by the seventh-century Sandwich stone. It probably represents the name of the runemaster, Ræhæbul, and was originally part of the interior of a grave. The text, as best it can be made out, can be read in figure 1.16.

Among the manuscript uses of the runes, the one most approaching magical practice is the concealment of secret meanings in texts through the use of runes. One such text is found in Riddle 19 of the *Exeter Book*,[1] which translated from OE would read:

> I saw a ᛋᚱᚩᚻ (horse) with a bold mind and a bright head, gallop quickly over the fertile meadow. It had a ᚾᚩᛗ (man), powerful in battle, on its back, he did not ride in studded armor. He was fast in his course over the ᚪᚷᛖᚹ (ways) and carried a strong ᚳᚩᚠᚩ ᚪᚻ (hawk). The journey was brighter for the progress of such as these. Say what I am called . . .

Here, the runes spell out words, but they are written *backwards* in the text. So the runic words read *hors* (horse), *mon* (man), *wega* (ways), and *haofoc* (hawk). However, and this is a remarkable and mysterious thing, the

[1] For the original text see Frederick Tupper (ed.) *The Riddles of the Exeter Book* (Boston: Ginn, 1910): 14–15. The translation here is my own. See also Paul F. Baum (trans., ed.), *Anglo-Saxon Riddles of the Exeter Book* (Durham, NC: Duke University Press, 1963).

individual *rune names* were to be read in the order as written so that the poem would have its proper alliteration.

Frisian Runestaves

No Frisian Futhork exists, but we do have a small body of interesting inscriptions. There have been about sixteen genuine Frisian monuments found so far (there are also a number of fakes). They date from between the sixth and ninth centuries. These inscriptions are generally found on wooden or bone objects that have been preserved in the moist soil of the Frisian *terpens* (artificial mounds of earth engineered in the marshes as an early form of land reclamation).

Frisian runic monuments seem to have a distinctly magical character, but many of them are difficult to interpret. We can be sure that they occur in a solid pagan context because this conservative region, often under the leadership of heroic kings such as Radbod, resisted the religious encroachment of the Christians—along with the political subversion of the Carolingian empire—until the late seventh century. We can even safely assume a period of reluctant religious compliance until long after that.

One of the most interesting, if difficult and complex examples of these Frisian pieces is the "magic wand" or talisman of Britsum (figure 1.17), which was found in 1906 and which dates from between 550 and 650. The wand is made of yew and is about 5 inches long. Side A of the inscription

Figure 1.17. Wand of Britsum

reads from left to right: *thin ī a ber!* *et dudh*; side B can be read from right to left: *biridh mī*. The damaged part of the piece cannot be read. The whole formula is translated "Always carry this yew [stave]! There is power [*dudh*] in it. I am carried. . . . " It might be pointed out that the seven-point dividing sign on side B indicates the seventh rune following the marker; that is, : | : (in this inscription) = : ↑ : yew—the power contained in the formula.

Viking Age Runes
(800-1100 C.E.)

As with all historical epochs, the Viking Age was not a sudden development but rather the result of a long, continuous process that had begun in the last centuries B.C.E. with the first movements of the Cimbri and Teutones from Scandinavia—that "Womb of Nations," as the Gothic historian Jordanes called it.

In the years around 800 Scandinavia was undergoing a number of internal changes and taking new directions. Sweden (especially Gotland) had already begun to develop the trade routes to the east among the Slavs, routes that would eventually reach Byzantium, Baghdad, and Persia. In Denmark powerful kings (Godfrid and Horik) were beginning to shape the Danish "nation" by mustering vast armies and mighty retinues. Norway, however, in its isolated and geographically fragmented condition, held to more local institutions and conservative ways. Although parts of Sweden (Uppland and Gotland) and certain areas in the Danish archipelago had long been wealthy, the rest of Scandinavia was just beginning to accumulate wealth and to grow in new ways at this time. The first Viking raid was carried out by Norwegians in 793 on the monastery at Lindesfarne (Northumbria), followed by raids on Monkwearmoth (794) and Iona (795), all of which heralded the dawn of the Viking Age.

Figure 2.1. Common Nordic Futhark

Just as the historical Viking Age was the result of a long process, so too was the evolution of the Younger Futhark from the older one. An examination of Elder Futhark inscriptions and alternate forms of elder runes will show that stave forms that were to become standard in the Younger Futhark were already in use from about 600 c.e. The evolution from the elder to the younger *tradition* took place at a fairly rapid pace during the eighth century, so that by 800 the new, systematically formed Younger Futhark, reduced from twenty-four to sixteen staves, had been completed, institutionalized, and disseminated throughout all of the Scandinavian lands.

The Younger Futhark is a purely Scandinavian cultural phenomenon, although many inscriptions are found outside Scandinavia, mainly in the British Isles and in the east. All of these inscriptions were carved by Nordic runemasters.

It is quite certain that all of this development took place within a traditional cultic framework—otherwise the older alterations and the eventual reformation of the row would not have taken place in such a uniform fashion and be spread with such speed and precision over such a wide expanse. In many ways the history of the younger reformation runs parallel to the original formation of the elder tradition. One of the major contrasts, however, is the way in which staves of the younger Futhark were quickly altered (in some cases drastically) in certain regions. This may point to an increased fragmentation in the tradition, but the fact that it held onto its internal system of order (number), phonetic values, and *ætt* divisions, as well as to the traditional modes of use (i.e., *carving*, not writing), testifies to the strength of the deep-level tradition.

We can suppose that the original, reformed "Common Nordic" rune row appeared in the form we see in figure 2.1. However, the final and most standard version of the Futhark appeared in the slightly different form that we see in figure 2.2.

The development of this futhark was dependent on a combination of linguistic and magical criteria. But in discussing the role of linguistic change in the evolution of the younger row, it must be noted that the evidence shows this to be strictly secondary. The elder row could have been adapted easily (as indeed it has been earlier) to any sound changes that might have occurred in the language. But this was not done. Instead, as the language developed a more complex sound system, it simplified its writing system—an unheard of event in the history of orthography. This is accounted for by the fact that the reformation took place for extralinguistic, magico-religious reasons.

Before we get into the traditional evolution, it is important to recount some of the major linguistic changes and how they were reflected by the staves, so that a "grammar" of the inscriptions will be clearer. To begin with, the phonetic value of : ᛇ : had always been uncertain, and it rarely appeared except in magical formulaic inscriptions. Also, : ᛃ : alternating with : ᛄ : changed its phonetic value at an early date (ca. 600) in the north because an original initial *j* was generally lost in Nordic at that time. A neat example of this rule is provided by the rune name itself, where Germanic *jēra* became Primitive Norse *jār*, which developed into Old Norse *ár* : ᛅ :. Hence, the phonetic value of the stave goes from [j] to [a]. In addition, : ᚨ : went from [a] to a nasalized form [ą]. It is also important to notice the new ambiguity of the whole writing system, where many staves now have to represent two or more sounds (see Table 3 in the Appendix.)

The traditional elements indicate the continuity of the two systems, both elder and younger. These elements clearly show that the transition from one system to the other was carried out within a cultic framework and that the developers of the younger row had knowledge of the elder row and its

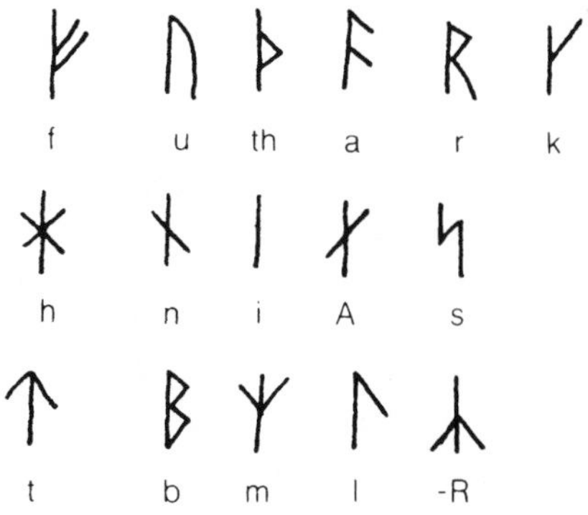

Figure 2.2. Standard Nordic Futhark

traditions. This conclusion is bolstered by the fact that all of this took place in what was essentially a nonliterate society. For although the runes were a form of writing, they had not yet been generally put to the task of simple and profane interpersonal communication. For one human being to be informed about a complex system of any kind (e.g., runelore) he had to be *told about it* by another human being. In those days the would-be runester could not go to a library and pick up a dusty tome about a long dead tradition and reanimate it.

The first element in this system is the continuity in the linear order of the staves, especially the first six: F-U-TH-A-R-K; otherwise, none of the staves of the Younger Futhark is displaced from its relative position in the elder row. Certain elder staves are dropped, and a new order emerges. The one exception to this rule is : λ : [-R], which is moved to the end of the whole row. This is perhaps due to the fact that it occurred only at the *ends* of words, but it also may have something to do with a conscious effort to preserve certain elements of the ancient *ætt* system. As we saw with regard to the elder period, the *ætt* system was an integral part of the elder tradition. (See chapter 9 for more esoteric aspects.) The continuity of this unusual feature is more evidence for the conscious manipulations of a cultic institution. The first *ætt* of the younger row is made up of the first six staves of the elder, in an unaltered order. It is also important that the second and third *ættir* begin with the same two staves as in the elder period, i.e., H–N and T–B, respectively. This, combined with the necessity of a symmetrical division following the mandatory sixfold first *ætt*, necessitated the movement of : λ : [-R] to the end; otherwise it would have caused the third *ætt* to begin with : h :. In any event, the continuation, and indeed strengthening, of the threefold grouping is a truly remarkable characteristic.

Simpler correspondences are nonetheless amazing. The level of continuity of stave forms is noteworthy: eleven forms remained unchanged, and three changed staves actually represent older alternate forms (i.e., : < :/ : Y :, : $\mathsf{\diamondsuit}$:/: $\mathsf{*}$:) and the virtually interchangeable : λ :/: Y :, which originally developed from a : X : form. That leaves only two that pose any problems at all; : M : became : Y :, and : H : became : $\mathsf{*}$:. These are explicable on formal grounds. The younger row generally made all double staves into single ones, so that by moving the head staves together, the new forms : Y : and : X : would emerge. The : f : was already an old unaltered form, so the modification : $\mathsf{*}$: was preferred. This latter form is also explicable on esoteric grounds (see chapter 10).

Another remarkable element is that of the continuity of the rune names and hence their primary phonetic values. Although we do not have any sources for the elder rune names, a combination of the comparative study of the languages in which the names do appear (i.e., OE, Go., and ON and the study of the *ideographic* use of the elder runes (see, for example, the ring of Pietroassa, on page 18) indicate that the later names are indeed a continuation of an age-old system. The Old Norse tradition preserves the names in rune poems (see chapter 8). The only apparent divergence is in the [-R] : ᛣ : *ýr*, " yew" (bow), from [-R] : ᛉ : *elhaz*, "elk." However, the elder alternate form : ᛉ : has been interpreted as originally having to do with tree symbolism (see the four cosmic harts [= elks?] in the limbs of Yggdrasill). Also, the second rune, : ᚾ :, has received a secondary meaning, "drizzling rain," which is explicable on mythical, cosmogonic grounds (see chapter 10).

It seems necessary to assign an original homeland to the Younger Futhark because it would be difficult to account for two simultaneously developing identical systems in both Norway/Sweden and Denmark. Based on the evidence, the most likely location for this phenomenon is extreme southern Norway and the adjacent Swedish region, where runic activity had remained strong through the end of the elder period. The time of this formation would have been the closing decades of the eighth century. From this location it quickly spread to Denmark. There it fell on fertile ground and began to revivify the runic tradition in the Danish archipelago. In Denmark it was slightly modified and became the most influential model for future runic development. This situation sprang from the general growth in Danish cultural and political influence in the region at this time.

All of this leads us to a discussion of the most common forms of the futhark actually codified in Viking Age Scandinavia. Despite the variations in the shapes of individual staves, they maintained a consistent inner structure and organization.

From the original codification in and around southern Norway and Sweden, the Younger Futhark spread to Denmark, where the codified forms were generally those found in figure 2.3. This Danish row was to become the most common of all futharks. It lasted from the ninth century to the eleventh and was the model for even later developments.

Figure 2.3. Danish Futhark

f u th a r k   h n i A s   t b m l -R

Figure 2.4. Rök Futhark

f u th   a   r   k   h n i A s t b m l -R

Figure 2.5. Hälsinga Futhark

The Danish Futhark was, howeer, quickly reformed in some areas on the Scandinavian peninsula. By 850, in southern Norway and in Östergötland, Sweden, a simplified row was developed, which can be seen in figure 2.4

This is generally known as the Rök row after the most famous inscription in this futhark, the Rök stone. These particular stave forms lasted only until the latter half of the tenth century, when they were again replaced by the more standard Danish type.

Besides these two main futhark styles in use during the Viking Age in Scandinavia, in Sweden there was the sporadic use of a radically simplified stave system, later called the Hälsinga runes (after the province in which they are found). These are generally formed by removing the head stave from the form. A futhark of such staves is shown in figure 2.5.

This row is rare in inscriptions, and it has been speculated that it was actually a runic shorthand used in more profane communications and for legal affairs. It might have been in use as early as the tenth century, but the most famous inscriptions date from the middle of the eleventh. Although the Hälsinga runes were never more than a local convention, it is noteworthy that they remained a part of the ancient tradition.

Viking Age Inscriptions

We can, for the most part, find every kind of inscription in the younger period that we found in the elder one, but the type that comes to predominate in the evidence we have is that of the memorial stone. This is due in part to its durable character. However, talismans of various kinds remain an important part of the record as well. To date, around 5,000 younger runic monuments of all types have been found, but this number continues to grow as Viking Age settlements are excavated.

RUNIC MEMORIAL STONES

The tradition of carving, first, gravestones (very often found *within* the grave with a direct magical function), and later, memorial stones with apparent magical import dates back to the elder period. The *bauta* stones were, of course, closely connected to the grave. The younger tradition seized on this idea and made it a mainstay of its work. In the younger period such stones were not necessarily so closely associated with the grave itself, and therefore they are better referred to as memorials. This tradition began in Denmark around 800. It should be noted that this new bursting forth of revivified runic practice coincided with the reception of the reformed futhark and historically in connection with the ideological threat from Christianity in the south.

A famous example of an ancient form of gravestone, which actually represents the transition between the *bauta*- and memorial-stone types, is found on the stone of Snoldelev (see figure 2.6). This stone, which dates from between 800 and 825, was probably originally placed within the grave mound, but its formula bears some resemblances to the later memorials. It is also interesting to note that the stone was used for cultic purposes as early as

Figure 2.6. Snoldelev stone

the Bronze Age (ca. 1500–500 B.C.E.). We know this because a sun-wheel sign is still barely visible (with proper lighting) on its face (see dotted lines on figure 2.6). Its inscription is to be transliterated:

kun uAltstAin sunaR
ruhalts thulaR asalhauku (m) [?]

which can be translated: "Gunvald's stone, the son of Rohald, the *thulr* [= cultic speaker in the cult of Ódhinn] at Salhaugen."

Snoldelev is especially interesting for its testimony concerning an official title within the Ódhinic cult (the ON *thulr* and the OE *thyle*), which has to do with the role of the magician/priest as a cultic reciter of law, incantation, mythic song, and the like—and the powerful holy signs, the three interlocked drinking horns (a symbol of the Ódhinic cult) and the solar-wheel/swastika. (Note the relationship between the later solar wheel and the older sun-wheel sign.)

A more classic example of the memorial-stone tradition is provided by the great Strö stone from near the village of Strö in southern Sweden (Skaane). The stone dates from about 1000 and was originally part of a grave-mound complex of seven stones (two with runic inscriptions). Although the mound has since fallen in, this was one of the first runic monuments to be described by Ole Worm in 1628.

The staves, which can be read in figure 2.7, are executed within a zigzag, serpentine ribbon.

This inscription would be rendered in Old Danish as *Fadhir lét hoggva rúnaR thessi øftiR Azzur bródhur sínn, es norr vardh dødhr í vikingu* and translated: "Father had these runes cut after [= in memory of] his brother Asser, who died up in the north while a-viking."

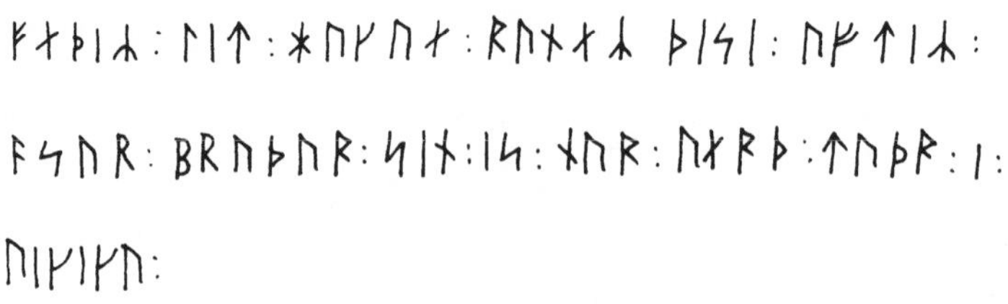

ᚠᛅᚦᛁᛦ:ᛁᛁᛏ:ᚼᚾᚠᚾᛏ:ᚱᚾᛅᛏᛅ ᚦᛁ�747ᛁ:ᚾᚠᛏᛁᛅ:

ᚠ�47ᚾᛦ:ᛒᚱᚾᚦᚾᛦ:ᚼᛁᛏ:ᛁᚼ:�423ᚾᛦ:ᚾᛅᚱᚦ:ᛏᚾᚦᛦ:ᛁ:

ᚾᛁᚠᛁᚠᚾ:

Figure 2.7. Inscription of Strö

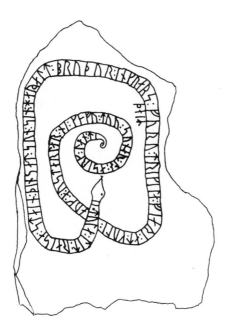

Figure 2.8. Gripsholm stone

The Strö stone clearly shows the memorial characteristics of these monuments. A few technical observations are in order also. Note that often double letters are not indicated by the staves (ᚼᚢᚴᚢᛅ =*hoggva*); : ᛅ : can stand for *-ng-*, as well as other ambiguities in the orthography of the inscription.

This stone shows us how these monuments were carved in memory of Viking raiders who died in foreign lands, which apparently was quite common. It also gives testimony to the fact that (professional?) runemasters were engaged for the carving of the staves.

A possible mytho-magical example of such a memorial stone is magnificently provided by the stone of Gripsholm. This stone commemorates a "brother of Ingvarr" who fell with the mythic hero (Ingvarr) while in the east. The outlines of the Gripsholm stone, which dates from the middle of the eleventh century and measures 6 feet by 4 feet 6 inches, are given in figure 2.8 on page. Its inscription, beginning at the head of the serpent, should be transliterated as follows:

tula: lit: raisa: stain: thinsat: sun: sin: haralt: bruthur: inkvars:
(thaiR) furu: trikila: fiari: at: kuli: auk: a: ustarlar: ni: kafu: tuu:
sunar: la:
asirk: lan: ti.

The latter part of the formula is in verse, and the whole may be translated:

Tola had this stone raised for his son Harald, Yngvarr's brother.
[They] fared boldly
far away after gold
and in the east
they gave [food] to the eagle;
they died in the south
in Serkland.

(Note that the double-point dividing signs, which usually indicate the divisions between words, are sometimes used within words. There may be some magical encoding at work here.)

More than thirty stones from this region (around Lake Mälar) and time period refer to men dying in the east with Yngvarr. Here we are probably dealing with a ritualized mythicizing of the deaths of men who fell in Russia and beyond during the later Viking Age. The Yngvarr to which these stones refer is supposed to be a historical figure who launched a great expedition against the Islamic world in the east—Serkland—around 1040. ("Serkland," which means either "shirt-land" or "silk-land," is sometimes more narrowly identified with Persia.) However, there is no evidence to show that this particular expedition ever took place. This, coupled with the fact that this Yngvarr (sometimes spelled Ivar) had the same curious nickname (*vídhfadhmi* [far-traveler, or wide-fathomer]) and the same theater of demise (Serkland) as a semimythical Yngvarr (who would have lived in the sixth or seventh century) tend to make us believe that at one point all of those slain in the east were ritually said to have "fallen with Yngvarr," a heroic figure from the mythicized past. The mythical Yngvarr is mentioned in the *Heimskringla*, and a whole medieval Icelandic saga is devoted to him.

The poetic lines of the inscription are interesting because they testify to an ancient and sacred formula—*erni gefa* (to give [sacrifice] to the eagle)—as a way of expressing the sacral nature of battle in connection with the Ódhinic cult.

Talismanic Objects

A wide variety of object types continued to be transformed into talismans in the Viking Age and beyond. Many were pure talismans (see Kvinneby below), whereas others were utilitarian objects turned into talismanic ones by means of loading them with rune might. The famous ship burial of Oseberg (late-ninth-century Norway), perhaps the grave of queen Asa, included two runic inscriptions—one on a bucket and one on a round stake (beechwood, about 8 feet long) of uncertain function. It was probably part of the steering mechanism of the ship. The inscription, which is executed in Norwegian/Swedish (Rök) runestaves, can be read in figure 2.9.

This formula requires a good deal of runic knowledge to read. Nevertheless a literal meaning can be extracted:

Litil(l)-víss m(adhr)

The last stave is used ideographically to stand for its name, and the entire text can be translated: "[the] man is little wise," or "[a] man [who] knows little," the significance of which is to ward off the uninitiated from the deeper meaning of the inscription.

This deeper meaning is concealed by the common technique of stave scrambling. In this case it hides the famous magical formula *mistil*, which shares significance with the word *mistletoe* (ON *mistilteinn*), the twig of the little mist. Note that the latter part of the *mistil* formula is repeated twice, as is the other part of the formula, *vil* (= ON *vél* [craft]).

```
l  i  t  i  l  u  i  s  m -and- l  i  t  i  l  u  i  s  m
9  8  4  5  6  7  2  3  1        6  5  4  8  9  7  2  3  1
```

Figure 2.9. Oseberg formula

ᚺᚢᚾᛏᚱᚤᛄᛁᚱᛁ ᛈᛏᚱᛏᛈᛏ ᛁᛈᛃᛖᛐᛩ ᚤᚱᛏᛏ
ᛏᛏ ᛚᚱᛏ ᛏᛏ ᛁ

Figure 2.10. Lund weaving temple formula

So the secret inscription would read:

mistil-til-vil-il or simply *mistil-vil*

In standard Old Norse this would be *mistil-vél*, the craft of the little mist—the magical powers over life and death. References to this magical mythos can be found in the story of the death of Baldr.

Another talismanic inscription on a utilitarian object is found on the weaving temple of Lund (Sweden), from about 1000 C.E. This interesting runic text gives us a sample of the curious mixture of love and curse magic, and the common blending of the two in Nordic sources. For other examples from the literature, see the "Skírnismál" (stanzas 25–36) in the *Poetic Edda* and the confusion between the two forms found in *Egil's Saga*, chapter 72. The runic text of the temple can be read in figure 2.10.

In more standardized form: *Sigvarar Ingimar afa man min grat*, which can safely be translated "Sigvör's Ingimarr will have my sorrow," is then followed by an eight-stave magical formula: *aallatti*. The effect of the inscription is strengthened by the hidden numerical pattern of twenty-four staves in the main formula and eight in the auxiliary rune *galdr*. The purpose of the inscription is clear: it is to cause the husband (or fiancé?) of Sigvör (who is named Ingimarr) to have the runecarver's lovesickness; that is, he will lose Sigvör in some manner so that the runester can have her.

The final example of a talismanic object from the Viking Age is the copper plate (about 2 inches square) of Kvinneby (Öland), which dates from the late eleventh century. This is truly remarkable amulet, the complexities

Figure 2.11. Kvinneby bind runes

of which we cannot fully explore in this space. Its fairly long text (144 staves) is inscribed in nine rows of *boustrophedon* (as one plows a field; i.e., from left to right and then back from right to left, etc.). This was a continuous practice in runic inscriptions from the elder period. The text is preceded by six magical bind rune staves (the first of which has been obliterated). These bind runes can be seen in figure 2.11. These signs are followed by the runic text itself, which can be translated as follows:

Glory to thee I bear,
Bofi. Help me! Who
is wiser than thou? And bear all
in evil from Bofi. May Thórr protect
him with that hammer that from
the sea came, (it) flew from evil. Wit
fares not from Bofi. The gods are
under him and over h-
im.

This is followed by a schematic drawing of a fish.

What is important to notice in the surface meaning of this talisman is the use of mythic imagery to shape the magical charge. In this case it is the protective power of Thórr—his hammer, Mjöllnir—which always returns from the source of "evil" once it has hit its mark. Also, the image of the gods surrounding the shielded man, above and below, is significant in that it shows the gods present below as well as above. The Old Norse word that is usually translated as "evil" is *illr*, which keeps to its original primary meanings "ill, oppressive, difficult, mean (things)," and so on, rather than its later Christian meaning that indicates an absolute moral force.

Runic Technology

An often ignored aspect of runology is that of the materials and techniques used in the actual production of runic objects. This is one area where "experimental archeology" can be of great value, which in turn can lead to a deeper understanding of the inner realms of the runes. Most of what is said here is valid for both the elder and younger periods.

We know certain things about the way in which they were executed by the runemasters from the runic inscriptions themselves. For example, besides the obvious physical evidence, we know from the runic terminology that rune staves were *carved* into the surfaces of various substances. The most common term in regard to this is Germanic *wrītu* (I carve), which eventually becomes Primitive Norse *ristan* (to carve). These terms are related to the English "write." However, the original sense was that of carving or cutting.

The tools with which these carvings were made are generally unknown to us, so we can only guess at their nature. The famous stone of Eggjum tells us that it was not scored with an iron knife (*ni sakse stAin skorin*). Therefore, we know that for certain purposes there was probably a prohibition against using iron in cutting runes, but we also know that many objects must have been carved with iron knives. Here we are most certainly dealing with the elemental science of runecraft. The great runestones of the Viking Age were surely carved by means of a hammer and chisel after they had been dressed with a pick and/or ax. Some inscriptions may have even been executed by means of a pick hammer, tapping away at the surface along the lines of the staves. The stone of Snoldelev seems to have been done in this way. Other kinds of tools used in magical inscriptions were knives (see *Egil's Saga*, chapter 44) and needle-like objects (which must have been used to cut inscriptions such as the Kvinneby amulet). Some of these needles may have been crafted from nonferrous metals (bronze, copper, etc.) or from nonmetallic substances (e.g., bone or stone).

The physical evidence also bears ample witness to the substances into which runes were carved. Furthermore, the epigraphic and literary terminology of runelore gives us clues to the relative frequency with which various materials were employed. Wood was clearly the medium of choice among the runemasters. Terms for the runes themselves generally revolve around wood and not any other runic medium. Very often the word *stave*, which literally means "stick" or "staff," is used as a synonym for *rune*. We get our English word *stave* from the plural form of *staff* (ON *stafr*). This points to the fact that originally the figures representing the mysteries were carved onto small wooden sticks (used in magic and divination) and that a shift in meaning took place in which the most popular mode of representing the rune became a synonym for the concept itself. Although this connection must go back to the era of runic origins, the oldest example of "stave" standing for "rune" is on the now lost stone of Gummarp (ca. 600 c.e.), which reads:

HAthuwolAfA
sAte
stAbAthria
ᚦᚦᚦ

This can be translated as "Hathuwulf set three staves: ᚦᚦᚦ ."

Not only did the "stave" come to stand for the sign of the rune, but it eventually took on all the meanings of the word *rune* itself, so that in Old Norse we find *stafr* (more usually in the plural, *stafir*), meaning not only "staff, stick, post" but also "lore, secret lore, wisdom, magical sign." Runic terminology was so well entrenched in the languages that in many dialects the vocabulary of Latin letters was reshaped by it. In Old Norse, written letters are referred to as *stafir*, and even the complex magical signs (ON *galdrastafir* [magical staves]) use this term even though they are sometimes drawn with pen and ink. Old English *stæf* (letter, writing) and Old High German *stab* (stave, letter) are also examples of this. Note the modern German word for "letter" *Buchstabe* vs. *Stab* (stick, stave, wand).

Another often neglected yet essential aspect of runic technology, which is nevertheless important to modern runecraft, is that of coloring the staves and the objects on which they are carved. Again, the elder inscriptions themselves tell us that the staves were indeed colored, by frequent use of the verb *fāhidō* (I colored, or painted). The later Old Norse vocabulary continued to use the descendant of this Germanic verb form, *fá*, in the same context. Moreover, we know that the most popular color for the runes themselves was red (made with red oxide of lead, minium, or most often, ochre). This was generally a magical substitute for blood (see *Egil's Saga*, chapter 44). Comparative historical linguistics gives us good evidence for the magical importance of the color red for the Germanic peoples. The Old English *teafor* is an old term for red ochre, but the word is also found in Old High German as *zouber* (magic, divination) and in Old Norse as *taufr* (talismanic magic, talisman). It seems that one of the old ways "to do magic" was "to make red [with ochre]" some symbolic object in conjunction with a transference of magical might. This technique is made very clear in the passage from *Egil's Saga* cited above.

Other colors that were used, especially on later runestones, were black (made with soot) and white (a lime solution), as well as blue and brown. Traces of some of these have been found on the stones themselves. The Viking Age runestones were not originally the gray objects we might see today but brightly colored blazing beacons on the landscapes of all the worlds.

The coloring was used in a variety of ways. Its original function was undoubtedly magical. However, this was multileveled. The runes were stained a different color from the background (often red on white or black), which made the stave stand out. Furthermore, colors were used to make word divisions, with every other word (or part of speech) in a different color. There is also evidence that some runes were not actually cut into the stone but only *painted* in place! This opens up the possibility of an enormous number of forever lost runic documents that were just painted on the surfaces of rocks or wooden objects—all long since washed or blown away.

The language of the Viking Age inscriptions is generally referred to as Old Norwegian, Old Swedish, or Old Danish, depending on the dialect area in which it was produced. However, those with a knowledge of the literary forms of Old Norse, coupled with some basic runology, would have little trouble in deciphering runic texts found on Viking Age runestones. This is because the Norse dialect remained quite homogeneous until around 1000; then East Norse (Swedish and Danish) and West Norse (Norwegian and Icelandic) began to develop. But even then the changes remained relatively minor through the close of the Viking Age.

3

Medieval Runes
(1100-1600 C.E.)

The Viking Age was drawing to a close around 1050, and by 1100 the period characterized by the vigor of the Viking raids was over. Christianity was becoming the official cult of the courts and eventually of most of the people. But we know from historical sources for this complex period that the Christianity they practiced was in many cases not really orthodox, and in fact their religion represented a kind of mixed faith of Ásatrú and Christianity.

Denmark had officially become Christian in the late tenth century; and although the Norwegians maintained a long struggle against the alien creed and political structure, Norway was officially secured by the Christian camp by the early eleventh century. In Sweden the story is more complex. There apparently had been a number of Christians in Sweden (Irish slaves who did not abandon their ways) from the early Viking Age, and various missionary expeditions sent into the country during the eleventh century exposed pagan ideas to many Christian formulas that found their way into heathen practice. But Sweden did not officially become Christian until around 1100.

In this period of tenuous and irregular beginnings much of the organized tradition of the runic cult was destroyed along with its larger religious framework. However, a number of factors, such as the comparative lack of Christian indoctrination of the Scandinavian clergy, a historically tolerant attitude, and the remoteness of the whole region compounded by the in-

accessible outback districts, combined to make fertile ground for the survival of runic traditions among the farmers and lesser nobility.

During the Catholic period the runes were brought into the service of
the Church itself—or so it would seem. However, this was somewhat of an
unholy alliance because the medieval runemasters were still largely in
possession of the elder lore, albeit in a fragmented state. Magic was still their
principal function, although they were also increasingly used in profane
communication. But without an organized cultus in support of the runic
tradition, it steadily declined throughout this period. However, the kernels
of the tradition were preserved through rote formal learning of names and
forms, sometimes in the context of profane writing. This process was carried
out unconsciously in all parts of what had been greater Germania, and we
will see evidence of this throughout our discussions. Besides this disparate
formal survival—guided by the web-work of wyrd—the indwelling runic
patterns survived as the "blood" of the ancient Erulians still coursing in our
veins. The mysteries are virtually encoded in the patterns of what might be
called our "collective unconscious."

The Reformation, which began in Sweden in 1527 and officially a bit
later in Norway/Denmark in 1536, brought both blessings and a terrible
curse. The blessings generally came about because of the growth in Swedish
nationalism and "racial consciousness" in the middle of the sixteenth century
that promoted all aspects of indigenous culture. The doctrines of *storgotic-*

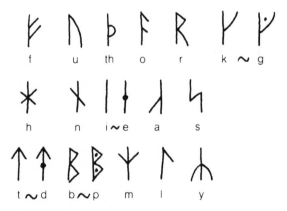

Figure 3.1. Dotted futhark

ism were formulated from widespread beliefs by the last Catholic archbishop of Uppsala, about 1554. The curse came with the wave of intolerance that followed after the Protestant wave had been absorbed. This resulted in the persecution of all practitioners of the old ways, especially those of the peasant class and country folk.

The ambiguity of the sixteen-stave row developed in the Viking Age posed little difficulty to the initiated runemaster and served very well for esoteric practices because it remained organically within the systematic runic structure. However, as the level of training slipped, the ambiguity of the sixteen-stave row was somewhat altered by the introduction of "dotted runes" (ON *stungnar rúnar*) beginning as early as the end of the tenth century in Denmark. At first this was an occasional addition of a point to clear up any possible ambiguity in the inscription. Although this practice makes it obvious that "profane" interpretations of the runes were assuming more importance, for at least two hundred years more the sixteen-stave row, sometimes in the "dotted" form, was the rule.

These dots were placed on or near the stave to distinguish it phonetically from its contrasting opposite in a natural class, for example, b:p, t:d, k:g (distinguished from one another by *voicing*). The oldest dotted runes with their phonetic values appear in figure 3.1.

This development became more "Latinized" until it was finally codified during the reign of Valdemar the Conqueror (1202–1241), when a true "runic *alphabet*" was formulated. That is, a stave was given for every letter in the Roman alphabet as it had been adapted for writing the contemporary Scandinavian dialects.

In Norway the thirteenth and fourteenth centuries saw the runic alphabet shown in figure 3.2 in general use. A similar thing happened throughout Scandinavia, including Iceland, during the Middle Ages, where a little after 1100 Ari inn Fródhi and Thóroddur Rúnmeistari created an expanded standardized *Futhorkh* to compete with the Latin script.

a b c d th e f g h i/j k l   m n o p r   s   t u/v x y   z æ ø

Figure 3.2. A runic alphabet

Medieval Inscriptions

In this epoch we begin to see many more different uses and depictions of runes and rune magic. Many of the old traditions continued in some conservative areas, while new uses of the runes, often replacing Latin letters, were introduced. Also, stories *about* runes and rune magic abound in thirteenth- and fourteenth-century Iceland, where we can be sure the runes were indeed used in arcane arts.

The memorial runic *bauta* stones continued to be a lively tradition on Gotland until after 1700! And although they were superficially Christianized, there remained much in them, both in their symbology and in their deeper structure, that reminds us of the old way. It is probable that those with knowledge of esoteric runelore were also not unwise concerning their hidden meanings at this time.

The "holy signs" (ideographic symbols) that would appear on these stones often seemed to have a mixed significance. The cross was usually equal-armed and sometimes appeared with a solar wheel in its midst, as shown in figure 3.3.

This motif, and elaborations on it, was continued until the end of the period in question. It has been speculated that this kind of cross was a substitute for the *ægishjálmr* (helm of awe) sign that had appeared in similar contexts in the heathen period. A typical example of the post-Christian *bauta* stone is provided by the Upplandic Morby stone (figure 3.4). It follows a peculiar tradition that developed at this time (early in the Christian period, ca. 1050–1150) of building a bridge for the dead relative and raising a memorial stone that also makes reference to the bridge—all of this being done for the sake of the dead one's soul (ON *önd* or *sál*). The staves of the Morby stone can be transliterated:

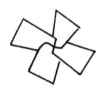

Figure 3.3. Solar wheel/cross sign

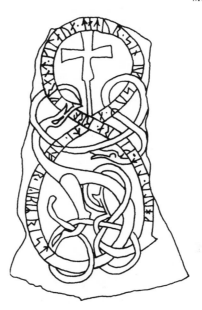

Figure 3.4. Morby stone

khulu lit kira bra f(u)rant kilau[h]a tatur sin[a] uk sum ati ulfr übir
risti

These runes are easily translated: "Gudhlaug had this bridge built for the soul [ant = *önd*] of Gillaug her daughter whom Ulfr had married. Øpir carved [the runes]." The stone is "signed" by Øpir, one of the most famous runemasters of history.

The practice of making runic talismans (*taufr*) continued into the modern era, and they were certainly popular throughout the medieval period. But because they were often carved in wood (and usually on very small pieces) and increasingly were being *written* on parchment, very few of them survive. Also, runemasters sometimes would destroy the talismanic objects once their work was done, and many were destroyed because of the post-Reformation persecutions of magical runemasters.

An example of a magical talismanic object from the medieval period is provided by a rib bone (ca. 30 inches long) that was found in the old church at Särkind, Östergötland, Sweden, and which dates from the fifteenth century. This bone probably functioned as a *göndr* (magical wand), and it bears the complex inscription seen in figure 3.5 on page 50.

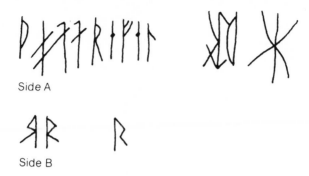

Side A

Side B

Figure 3.5. Wand of Särkind

The first part of side A is to be transliterated thaet tae refen (this is the rib bone). The second complex is made up of a manifold bind rune of uncertain meaning. It could conceal the name of the magician, or it could be a combination of certain runes for magical effect. This side of the inscription is concluded with a bold *hagall* rune, which in the esoteric school of this period would have had well-developed cosmic significance as the image of the World Tree and the seed of the multiverse. The three R-staves on side B are intended to formulate and guide the magical power generated by the vitki, as is clear from the esoteric lore surrounding the : ᚱ :.

Besides these archaic and sacred uses of the runes, they were also being employed in new and profane ways in common communications. We know that this was increasingly the case throughout the thirteenth and fourteenth centuries as the late saga literature often mentions the sending of runic messages on *rúnakefli* (rune sticks). *Hákons saga Hákonarson* in the *Heimskringla* mentions this several times. But the greatest evidence for "runic correspondence" was found in the excavations of the dock district in Bergen, Norway, where dozens of these messages were actually found. Some are as simple as a "note" from a wife telling her husband to come home from the local tavern, and some are as intriguing as an example that dates from the early thirteenth century, which may be translated as follows:

> I want to ask you to leave your party. Carve a message to Olaf Hettusveinn's sister—she is in the nunnery at Bergen—and ask for advice from her and from her kinsmen, when you want to come to terms. You are surely less stubborn than the earl. . . .

This is followed by a set of staves that have not yet been satisfactorily interpreted but may be transliterated :atu:kena:nu:baetu. It is possible that the message carries an encoded secret meaning; however, on the surface this is clearly an appeal from a member of one party or faction to a member of another, asking the recipient to leave his side and come over to that of the sender, but this is to be done secretly through a third party (the woman in the convent).

Runestaves were also increasingly finding their way onto the written page. At first this was part of an effort by some (such as Ari and Thóroddur, mentioned above) to develop the runes as an alternative to the Roman alphabet. There were probably many manuscripts written in runestaves, but only one lengthy one remains to us, the so-called *Codex Runicus*. The staves, or runelike signs, also were used ideographically in some manuscripts, standing either for the rune name or for some other symbolic quality. In the *Codex Regius* (the MS that contains the *Poetic Edda*) : Y : is often used as a substitute for the word *madhr* (man). There were also many manuscripts that contained lines written in runestaves and several treatises on runes—for example, the one by the German scholar/monk Hrabanus Maurus. Also, the important evidence of the *Galdrabók* cannot be forgotten because it represents runes and runelike "staves," secret runes, and the like, firmly within a magical context.

The rune poems are prime examples of the use of runestaves in manuscripts, but we will examine them separately in chapter 8.

It is only in the manuscript of the Laws of Skaane (*Skaanske Lov*)—or as it is more descriptively known, the *Codex Runicus*—that any surviving attempt at a substitute of runestaves for Latin letters is found. The manuscript probably dates from the fourteenth century. Later attempts to "revive" the runes as a utilitarian script were carried out by antiquarians, some of whom were quite serious and virtually "neo-pagan" in their beliefs (see Johannus Bureus, on page 54).

Besides these uses, the runes were widely employed in the construction of "prim-staves" or "rim-stocks," which worked as perpetual calendars. These seem to have the nominally Christian function of computing festival days, but the fact that runes were almost exclusively used in the construction of these objects from at least the fourteenth century all the way into the eighteenth shows the eternally living nature of runelore in the Scandinavian lands.

Modern Runic History (1600-1945)

This age is, in the beginning, historically closely connected with the Age of the Reformation. However, there was also a growing and more formal difference evolving between the knowledge of the scholar, who consciously attempted to rebuild the structure of older lore, and that of the folk, who in constantly changing form preserved the lore unconsciously. The distinction between revival on the one hand and survival on the other was growing. Each hold their advantages and disadvantages.

Revivalists, even in this early time, went back to material from the Elder and Viking Ages and thus *could* have come into contact with the "purest" and most traditional forms; whereas the folk tradition was (as the *Galdrabók* shows) always ready and willing to assimilate foreign features and thus lost sight of the original system (e.g., Latinization in the runic "alphabet"). But the folklore was directly bound, unconsciously and imperfectly as it might be, to the seed-forms of the ancient world view, an advantage not enjoyed by the revivalist scholars. The latter had been educated in the "classical" tradition, indoctrinated with Judeo-Christian ideas, and initiated into a largely Hermetic school of magic. Therefore, their attempts at revival of the old way were inevitably shaped by their backgrounds in the newly established traditions. But the potential for going beyond this, directly to the oldest levels, was eventually made possible by their efforts and ground-breaking work.

The first great homeland of runic revival, after it had been relegated to the most remote rural regions and deepest level of the cultural hoard, is Sweden. Around 1600 Sweden was an emerging world power with great pride in her past and great plans for her future. The combination of the intellectual freedom granted to the Swedish intelligentsia (but certainly not to the folk) by the Reformation and the growing nationalism led to the canonization of an ideology known as *storgoticism* (megleogothicism). This ideology is probably rooted in concepts that reach all the way back to ancient times, and it first raised its head in the late 1200s, within a century after the "Christianization" of the Swedes. Storgoticism is wrapped up with the almost mythic proportions attained by the people called Goths. This has continued in many ways as the word and concept *Goth* or *Gothic* have taken on many different meanings. The first documented reference to this latter-day "Gothic mythology" in Middle Ages occurs in the records of a Church Council held in Basel in 1434, where the Spanish claimed precedence in a matter over the English because they (the Spanish) were identical with the Goths and therefore the elder nation. To this the Swedish replied that in such case Sweden held precedence because they were the original Gothic people and the main stem of that nation.

Storgoticism was eventually codified by Johannes Magnus, who was the last Catholic Archbishop of Uppsala, in his book *Historia de omnibus gothorum sveonumque regibus* (1554). As Johannes Magnus formulated it, storgoticism was firmly bound to Hebraic mythology. It was thought that Sweden was the first land to be settled after the Deluge by the descendants of Japhet. This type of mythology was common in Great Britain at the same time. Essentially, Magnus's mythic history was a preconditioned fantasy in which, for purposes of prestige, he connected the Swedes to the Hebrews and claimed that all of the wisdom of ancient times (such as that possessed by the Greeks) was actually taught to the world by the Swedes. Also, it was believed that the runic "alphabet" was the oldest script in the world (with the possible exception of Hebrew).

This mythology influenced the next generation of storgoticists, which was contemporary with the Reformation in Sweden and the development of that nation into a world power. The great reformer of storgoticism was Johannes Bureus or Johan Bure (1568–1652), who was a tutor and advisor of King Gustavus Adolphus. Storgoticism had become a virtual religion by that time, and the historical aspects had been refined by Johannes Messenius in his *Scondia Illustrata*. But our main interest is with Bureus.

Bureus was the first great runic revivalist. His scholarship was considerable, and one of his most important tasks was the collection and recording of runic inscriptions from all over Sweden. By the end of his life he had transliterated about one-fourth of the then known inscriptions. Bureus was made Antiquary Royal in 1630, after having had the chair in history at the University in Uppsala. In 1620 it was declared that all future holders of this chair were bound to learn "runic" (i.e., the old language that the runes were used to represent) and how to interpret the signs. Between 1599 and 1611 Bureus wrote three books on runes, including a small illustrated edition of inscriptions, his *Runarafst*, and a runic primer. Although Bureus's scientific work was considerable, it was largely superseded in his own lifetime by the Dane Ole Worm. But this scholarly work was only part of the importance of the runes for Bureus.

Soon after 1600 Bureus began to develop a system of what he called "adulrunes." In this system he began to use the runes for mysto-magical purposes. Although it is said that he originally learned of the runes from the peasants of remote Dalarna, Bureus evidently was not content with building on the folk tradition, and he began to apply runelore to the magical teachings with which he was already familiar—"Christian Kabbalism." The adulrune system was simply developed by analogy with the Hebrew lore of the *Seper Yetzirah* (which we know he read). It is still unclear how much the indigenous Germanic traditions (such as runelore) influenced the shape of "mainstream" medieval magic, but in any case by this time there was a basic theoretical framework that must be described as Christian and that was to a large extent distinct from the folk traditions. Bureus's main sources were Paracelsus and pseudo-Paracelsian writings (e.g., the *Liber Azoth* and the *Arbatel*), early Rosicrucianism, and the works of Agrippa von Nettesheim. His principal runic technique was a variation of *temura* (a Kabbalistic procedure involving the permutations of letters in a word to give a new, "revealed" meaning). Bureus believed that all knowledge had originally been *one*, and since the lore of the Goths represented by the runes was the oldest of all lore, he could gain access to inner knowledge by acquiring the ability to grasp the adulrunes. Bureus did not, however, consider himself to be a neo-pagan. Quite to the contrary, he considered himself a "true" Christian, and he believed that the worship of God and the mastery of the power of prayer were essential to success in his system.

In 1613 Bureus became more deeply engrossed in the esoteric aspects of his studies and was especially enthralled by apocalyptic speculations. By the early 1620s the local church authorities began to look askance at Bureus's heretical theories, but his royal connections protected him from any prosecution by the Church. He believed in the approaching Judgment Day so strongly that he divided all of his property among the poor in

1647—the apocalyptic year according to his calculations—and lived five more years supported by royal aid.

Bureus's work is important in two areas: (1) it was the beginning of scientific runology, and (2) it again used runes in sophisticated magical and philosophical work. But the predictable and unfortunate shortcomings of his efforts in the latter field are obvious.

The whole storgoticism movement had far-reaching political ramifications. On its tide of nationalism Gustavus Adolphus broke with the Catholics and began his nationalistic programs justified by the ideas of storgoticism. In the area of religion there seems to have been an elite gathered in high circles for whom the Reformation was a cover for the development of a "Gothic Faith." The office of the Antiquary Royal was the center of this new national religion, headed by Bureus and supported by the king.

The runes played an important role in the inner workings of this system, but they also were being touted for more practical reasons. Bureus developed a cursive runic script with which he hoped to replace the Latin. During the Thirty Years War a Swedish general, Jacob de la Gardie, wrote communications to his field commanders in runes as a kind of code.

As the power of Sweden waned and the Age of Enlightenment began, the doctrines of storgoticism and the theories of men such as Bureus lost favor with the establishment, and they again slumbered in darker and more remote corners.

The next breakthrough of runic investigation began in the European Romantic period, which began about one hundred years later, in the late eighteenth and early nineteenth centuries. Again its strongest representative, as far as genuine revivalism was concerned, was Sweden. There, in 1811, the *Gotiska Förbundet* (Gothic League) was formed by the poets and social reformers Erik Gustave Geijer and Per Henrik Ling. Their movement was essentially grounded in literature, although it was a serious attempt to quicken the ancient spirit.

On the other side of the coin, there was the continuing folk survival of runelore throughout Germania and her colonies. This was especially vigorous in Scandinavia, where runes and runic writing continued to be used for both everyday affairs as well as magical spells.

In Scandinavia and the North Atlantic isles, the runic alphabet survived as a writing system well into the twentieth century. This is especially true in remote regions such as Dalarna, Sweden, and Iceland. The runic alphabet remained purely runic until the middle of the eighteenth century, when Latin letters began replacing staves and it became a mixed script. Besides this writing system, the runes also were used in the construction of prim-staves or rim-stocks. These are perpetual calendars introduced into Scandinavia in the Middle Ages and were always carved into wood or bone. These calendars were a common form of time reckoning in the North well into the nineteenth century.

Knowledge of the runes was kept vigorous by folk traditions, and the lore and craft of the runes was preserved along with their more mundane uses. In more remote parts of the Scandinavian peninsula there were rune-singers who could perform magical acts through *galdr*, and in Iceland magical practice involving runes and *galdrastafir* (often runelike magical signs) continued at least into the seventeenth century. At this folk level, as well as at the scholarly level, as we have just seen, elements of "establishment magic" (i.e., Judeo-Christian) quickly spread throughout the system and was happily syncretized into it. But those who have studied the sixteenth-century *Galdrabók* (which was used and added to in the seventeenth century as well) will know that the underlying methods remained virtually the same as in the native tradition.

In the southern Germanic areas there is some hard evidence for a similar tradition of runic survival. One of the most interesting examples of this is found in the Black Forest region of Germany in the so-called *Heidenhäuser* (heathen houses!). These are very old farm buildings in which the threshing floor and other parts of the hose are decorated with magical ideographs, some of which are of undoubted runic origin. Some of these are single runes, for example, ◊ ⋈ ⋩ Y ✳ ✝ ⋏ ⴿ ↑ , whereas others are bind runes or holy signs, for example, ✕ ⅌ ⊗ ⵚ ⵚ ⼻ ⵚ ✕ ⴷ. The buildings in which these signs appear mostly date from the late sixteenth to the early eighteenth centuries. It is probable that the signs were carved by a certain group of "initiates" who still knew the symbols and how to work their magic.

Similar magical signs have been found in the Harz region of Germany, and if we can believe some investigators, a wide range of medieval symbolism had its roots in runic shapes. But not only did the mere shapes survive—so did the essential lore surrounding them. However, as far as Germany and most of the rest of northern Europe are concerned, the events of 1914 to 1918 and 1939 to 1945 destroyed the remainder through death and the rending of the social fabric. The darkest hour is before the dawn.

Not only do we find survivals of this type in Europe but America also is not without her runic heritage. Here we are not speaking of the highly controversial "American runestones" but rather of the living magical traditions of the Pennsylvania "Dutch" (Germans). In the eighteenth century these settlers brought a rich magical heritage, the major tool of which is the "hex sign." This term is perhaps derived from an early misunderstanding of

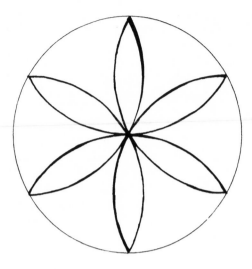

Figure 4.1. Hex sign pattern

the German *Sechszeichen* (six sign), so called because the earliest and most common signs were designed around the sixfold star or cross in the form seen in figure 4.1.

The word *hex* could be just as old because this term comes from the old Germanic sacred vocabulary and originally had to do with the "sacred enclosure" and the people (especially women) who practiced their arts there.

Such hex signs are virtual Germanic *yantras* and are used for every possible magical purpose. The sign is painted in bright colors on a round disk (usually of wood) and placed in locations significant to the working—outside on a barn or house, inside a house, or even carried on the person as an amulet. Again we see an important social aspect to this tradition. Hex signs can be effectively made only by an initiated *Hexenmeister*, and the work must be accompanied by an incantational formula. One formula known in South Carolina even calls on Thórr! There are indeed many dark and little known corners of this aspect of American history that deserve more work in our field.

Practitioners of the folk tradition remain unconscious of the historical details of their past and continually re-create the system according to their needs and conditions. This process is indeed the natural and healthy one; but when the folk tradition becomes "tainted" with an ideology hostile to it, this process becomes less effective as the life is slowly drained from it. Due to these circumstances it became necessary to develop new tools to dig out the lost life and lore of the elder heritage. The spirit necessary to this task was reborn in the early nineteenth century in northern Europe under the banners of literary Romanticism and academic philology. When it was discovered in the late eighteenth century that the languages of India and Europe were somehow organically related, a great school of thought arose in northern Europe, especially in Germany, that sought to put the study of these languages and cultures on a scientific basis. This came in the Age of Romanticism—which in many respects is a misnomer because in northern "Roman-ticism" people generally were looking more to Germanic models and away from those of classical antiquity. Perhaps a better term would be "German-ticism." In any event, serious interest in things Germanic, their origins, and their relationships to the greater Indo-European world grew rapidly. The greatest contribution to this area was made by Jacob Grimm, who, along with his brother Wilhelm, set about studying a wide range of manuscripts and collecting folk tales. In the process they virtually founded the disciplines of historical linguistics, comparative religion and mythology, and folklore. By means of what is now called "Grimm's Law" it was shown how Germanic was regularly derived from Indo-European, and its relationship to other dialects in that group (e.g., Sanskrit, Greek, Latin) was demonstrated.

Together with linguistics, the religions expressed in the texts being studied—the *Eddas*, the *Vedas*, Homer, Irish sagas—and the names of the gods were being compared; and schools of thought concerning the ways to interpret the mythologies were developing. As might be expected, many of those theories seem rather naive today, but the road to reconstruction is by its very nature fraught with pitfalls. The details of this historical process are much too complicated to go into here, but we must mention two theories held by older investigators. One was the tendency to go for "naturalistic" interpretations, to see mythology as a pure reflection of natural phenomena, which we now know to be only a part of the mythological function. The second tendency, or controversy, was the oscillation between considering mythology to be the creation of an ancient priesthood or sovereign class and the idea that it was essentially an outgrowth of the tales of the simpler folk tradition. The recognition of this dichotomy was astute, and it was later to become an important concept.

The importance of this pioneer work is that it put the investigation of such matters on a scientific basis, which has as its foundation the careful study of existing evidence of all kinds. If this work is carried out in an objective yet sympathetic manner, the veils of negative (Christian) psychological conditioning are lifted, and the possibility of penetrating to the most archaic levels of ideology is offered.

The Magical Revival

It was not until the first years of the twentieth century that a magical runic revival began, but this revival had manifold roots and was itself many-faceted. The late nineteenth century also saw the emergence of spiritualism and occultism in popular culture. The most influential branch of this phenomenon was *Theosophy*, as formulated by Helena Petrovna Blavatsky and promoted through the Theosophical Society. Concurrent with this new interest in the occult was a strong revival of Germanicism, which also might be called Neo-Romanticism. This was coupled with the growth of political Pan-Germanicism following the unification of the German Empire in 1871.

All of these factors began to work together with the latest theories concerning mythology, religion, science (especially Darwinism), and philosophy. From this mighty mix emerged the heterogeneous *Deutsch-Bewegung* (Teutonic Movement). In every aspect the adherents of this movement had a practical bent. They were not out to philosophize from ivory towers, but rather it was their intention to alter the world in which they lived. They wanted to bring society back to its traditional (pre-Christian) roots—at least as they saw them. Even those who formally wished to think of themselves as "Christians" rejected most of what had traditionally been thought of as the Christian heritage and replaced it with Germanic mythology and folk tales. This branch of the movement generally went under the banner of the *Deutsch-Christen* (Teutonic Christians). But other, perhaps more honest members of this social revolution rejected the Christian tradition and again took up the standard of the All-Father.

As far as our central purpose of runic revival is concerned, the great figure of the age was *der Meister*, Guido von List (1848–1919). List was born into a well-to-do Viennese family with business interests. Although young Guido had a deep interest in the mystical and natural world from an early age and wanted to be an artist and scholar, he followed in his father's footsteps. Partly out of a sense of duty, it seems, he entered a career in business. It is said that when he was a boy of fourteen, he stood before a ruined altar in the catacombs of St. Stephen's Cathedral in Vienna and declared, "*Wenn ich einmal gross bin, werde ich einen Wuotans-Tempel bauen!*" ("When I get big, I will build a Temple to Wotan!"). During those early years, in the time he had free from his professional duties, List explored the alpine regions from his native Lower Austria to Switzerland. But in 1877 his father died, and he began to pursue more intensely his work as an artist, mystic, poet, and prophet. The years between 1877 and 1889 were difficult and obscure ones for List, but in the last of these years his two-volume novel *Carnuntum* appeared. This is a historical novel depicting the struggle between the Germanic and Roman cultures along the Danubian frontier—a favorite theme in his works. It was both a critical and a popular success.

During the next period of his life (1889–1891) List apparently devoted himself to study and inner work, for in the last year of this period a new phase began that shows evidence of initiatory insight. In 1891 he published his two-volume *Deutsch-Mythologische Landschaftsbilder* (Teutonic-Mythological Landscape Formations), which is a kind of geomantic investigation of the megalithic monuments, *tumuli*, earthworks, castles, and other sacred sites in Lower Austria; and a virtual catechism of his philosophy called *Das Unbesiegbare: Ein Grundzug germanischer Weltanschauung* (The Invincible: An Outline of Germanic Philosophy). Both of these works show signs of the elegance and ingenuity of his more systematic thought yet to come.

In German-speaking countries throughout these years the ideology expressed by Theosophy was quite influential, and although List's own relationship to the Theosophical Society itself is somewhat vague, he does seem to have been influenced in the direction of its philosophy and cosmology. *Der Meister* was, it seems fair to say, at least the equal of Madame Blavatsky in matters of this kind. It is a fact that many of the prominent Theosophists of the day were also followers of List.

Between 1891 and 1902 List's literary career was coming to a close—he had bigger things ahead of him—but this was his most successful period in literary endeavors. He produced several dramas and his second major novel, the two-volume *Pipara*.

The year 1902 was, however, the great turning point in the evolution of List's thought. In that year he underwent surgery for cataracts on both eyes. For eleven months he was virtually blind. During this time List seems to have undergone an initiatory experience, one that opened his inner eye to the secrets of the runes as expressed through the "Rúnatals tháttr Ódhins" in the "Hávamál" (see chapter 8). He began to investigate the Germanic past and its secrets with this newly won (or refined) ability. The years between 1902 and 1908, when the first book appeared in what was to become an encyclopedic series of works outlining his elegant system, were filled with great inner and outer activity. List was well connected with leading Pan-Germanic political figures and ideologies (e.g., Dr. Karl Lueger, the *Bürgermeister* of Vienna) as well as with many wealthy industrialists, all of whom supported his investigations into and actualization of the ancient Germanic mysteries. So in 1905, the Guido von List Gesellschaft (Society) was formed to underwrite the work of "the Master." In conjunction with this exoteric branch an esoteric inner group called the *Armanen Orden* was planned for initiatory work and the teaching of more occult practices.

In 1908 List's first book in his investigation series appeared, entitled *Das Geheimnis der Runen* (The Secret of the Runes), in which he postulates that the primal futhork was an eighteen-rune row. The original row was made up of a series of staves to which certain formulaic "kernel words" were attached. These kernel words, and variations on them, could then be used to decode any other word, ancient or modern, to get back to their original meaning in the "primal language" *(Ursprache)* itself.

Although there was a whole magical system attached to List's runic revelations, it remained largely secret until after his death—and much of it remains so today.

The rune book was followed in that same year by a general two-volume work—*Die Armanenschaft der Ario-Germanen* (The Armanism of the Aryo-Germanic People)—that outlined the ancient social structure and religion and pointed the way to its rebirth. Also in that year *Die Rita der Ario-Germanen* (The Sacred Law of the Aryo-Germanic People) appeared. (Here, *rita* is a term borrowed from Sanskrit *rta* or *rita*, cosmic order, law.) With this work List attempted to reestablish, on a religio-cosmic foundation, a Germanic basis for law and political structure.

The next year, 1909, saw the publication of *Die Namen der Volkerstämme Germaniens und deren Deutung* (The Names of the Tribes of the People of Germania and Their Interpretation) in which List applied his theories concerning the investigation of hidden significance in names and words through an analysis of the kernel syllables.

In 1910 he published *Die Bilderschrift der Ario-Germanen: Ario-Germanische Hieroglyphik* (The Symbol Script of the Aryo-Germanic People: Aryo-Germanic Hieroglyphics), which concentrated on the investigation of the esoteric significance of a wide range of symbol forms, including runes, glyphs (holy signs), and especially coats of arms. This work was compared to Blavatsky's *Secret Doctrine* by the famous theosophist (and member of List's group) Franz Hartmann in his journal *Neuen Lotusblüten* with the words. "The author has lifted away the thick veil, which covered the history of Germanic antiquity, and has given us deep insight into the Secret Doctrine of the ancient Germans and the meaning of their symbology."[1]

The most complex and comprehensive book in the series was *Die Ursprache der Ario-Germanen und ihre Mysteriensprache* (The Primal Language of the Aryo-Germanic People and Their Mystery Language). This did not appear in completed form until 1915, although sections of it had already been published as early as ten years before. The huge volume contains List's system of *kala*, of decoding words to reveal their hidden meanings. This system is a virtual science of folk etymology, which is very potent in magical practice but thoroughly disregards every rule of historical linguistics. The companion to this volume was to have been *Armanismus und Kabbala*. In this book List was to show the relationship between the two systems, and how the Kabbalah was actually *Armanen* wisdom that had been absorbed into Judeo-Christian thought and esoteric philosophy. However, in 1919, before the completed manuscript could be printed, List died, and the manuscript apparently was stolen—or kept secret by members of the *Armanen Orden*.

The grandiose ideology and religious philosophy expressed in List's works is far too complex to enter into in any detail here. But some of the principal ideas he articulated that have found their way into the runic revival in modern Vinland are (1) the "trifidic-triune triad," (2) the "bifidic-biune dyad" (*zweispältig-zweieinigen Zweiheit*), and (3) the historical concept of concealment of ancient lore and even sacred systems in apparently Christian or secular literature and symbology.

The idea of the bifidic-biune dyad resulted in the concept of a balance between spirit and matter and the idea that matter was actually condensed spirit.

However, List's formulaic use of *three* is the most prominent feature of his system. In many ways it prefigures the theories of G. Dumézil concerning the Indo-European tripartite socioreligious structure (see chapter 13). The kernel concept of List's triadic thought is the archetypal pattern of

---

[1] Franz Hartmann, "Review: Guido von List. Die Bilderschrift der Ario-Germanen: Ario-Germanische Hieroglyphik." *Neuen Lotusblüten* (1910): 370.

arising (birth), becoming/being (life), and passing away to new arising (death/rebirth). This paradigm is applied to a number of concepts to form an elegant religio-magical philosophy. First of all, it is applied to cosmological principles. But perhaps one of the most interesting applications is to a system of trilevel interpretation of myths or of any concept or symbol. In this system a concept is seen on (1) a common level—a popularly understood form, (2) the level of exoteric symbolism, and (3) the esoteric level. This puts any word or concept through a spiral of semantic permutations to reveal inner truths and hidden relationships.

The Guido von List Gesellschaft continued to flourish after the death of *der Meister*, as did dozens of other Neo-Germanic groups (not all of them having anything to do with rune knowledge). In the years before 1933 other investigators, such as Friedrich Bernhard Marby and Siegfried Adolf Kummer, began to teach some of the more practical aspects of runecraft (especially the use of runic postures—so-called "runic yoga"—and talismanic magic).

In order to understand the National Socialists' relationship to runelore, one must first realize the level of popularity such things had reached in the late nineteenth and early twentieth centuries. Runes and runelike forms had again become symbols (but often very "common" ones) of *Deutschtum*. Runology was not only a beloved topic of academicians, it also became a topic in which the layman could immerse himself.

The idea of a non-Judaic religious revival was also strong, and it ran the gamut from the "Teutonic Christians" (who replaced the Old Testament with Germanic lore and "Aryanized" Jesus) to the largely pagan organizations such as the Guido von List Society.

The roots of National Socialism are manifold, and we cannot enter into them in too much depth here. However, we can point to some of the uses and misuses to which the Nazis put the runes. We must also preface these remarks with the statement that whether it is runes or religion of which we speak, the *party-line* Nazi doctrine is usually anathema to the essence of true Germanic concepts and often the antithesis of kernel patterns of Odian philosophy and practice. There were, however, secret cells within high levels of the *Schutzstaffel* (SS) gathered around Heinrich Himmler, especially at the Castle of Wewelsburg in Westphalia, in which more open experimentation was practiced.

There can be little doubt that elements within these cells had a genuine interest in the establishment of a Germanic religious world view; however, the party leadership seems to have shown little real interest in this direction.

Table 4.1. Runic Symbols Used by National Socialists.

✳	*Lebensborn* (Spring of Life) program for racial eugenics
↑	*Hitler Jugend* (Hitler Youth) used this sign as a part of their badge.
ᛋᛋ	In tandem stood for the *Schutzstaffel* (SS), the "Protection Detachment."

But they were all masters of the magical forms of mass manipulation that involves the stimulation and activation of popular images and engineering them in such a way as to work one's will on the mass population. (Today we call it advertising, among other things.) One of the important steps one must take in using this process is the establishment of what might be called a meaning shift (or semantic shift) with regard to symbols. This is most effective when one takes an archetypally powerful symbol (e.g., ✛ or ᛉ) and fills it with a personalized significance (Jesus and Hitler, respectively). Some of the more common runic symbols used in the National Socialist movement are shown in table 4.1.

Soon after 1933, when the Nazis came to power, the various groups involved in the Germanic Renaissance outside the structure of the Party were outlawed. All of the work done by dozens of organizations and individual leaders was either absorbed into official Party doctrine, liturgy, and symbology or was submerged. F. B. Marby himself spent ninety-nine months in the concentration camp at Dachau.

What had not been destroyed in the years of consolidation of Party power between 1933 and 1938 was subsequently further damaged by the war itself. Not only did the war destroy individuals of great knowledge—it also ripped apart the social fabric all over Europe. The mass displacement caused by the hostilities and the socioeconomic revolutions that followed in Western Europe were probably the final blow to any vestiges of the folk tradition in the rural areas.

Indeed, it always seems that the darkest hour is before the dawn, and that holds true for the rebirth of our traditional ways. After the willful destruction of the traditions by the Church, and the often misguided distortions of political movements, the way is hard to bring the runic secrets back into the fabric of our culture—but this is a heroic challenge of our time.

Contemporary Runic Revival (1945-Present)

In the aftermath of World War II, interest in Germanic religion and in the runes was frowned upon in Germany, and to a certain extent even in academic circles, which had not gone untouched by "NS-runology." Although German esoteric runology within the context of Germanic religion had been virtually eliminated, it did find a new home in the more eclectic branches of Western occultism and in that most prestigious lodge of German occultism, the *Fraternitas Saturni* (Brotherhood of Saturn). Runic work based on the theories and practices of Guido von List, Friedrich Bernhard Marby, and Siegfried Adolf Kummer became a part of the magical curriculum of the Fraternitus Saturni chiefly under the guidance of Frater Eratus (Karl Spiesberger). Spiesberger's efforts, largely outlined in his two books *Runenmagie* (1955) and *Runenexerzitien für Jedermann* (1958), led esoteric runology in the direction of universalism and away from the *völkisch* interpretations. There is also a heavy admixture of Hermetic–Gnostic ideas, a trend already evident to a lesser extent with earlier rune magicians.

F. B. Marby, after his release from Dachau at the end of the war, again became active. But he was never able to gain the same level of achievement as he had during the earlier part of the century.

Runology in the context of a general Germanic revival began slowly. In 1969 Adolf and Sigrun Schleipfer reactivated the *Armanen Orden*. They also took over the leadership of the Guido von List Gesellschaft, which also had been dormant since the war. The new Grand Masters set about making the *Armanen Orden* a real working magical order with a foundation in Germanic mysticism. Other Neo-Germanic groups active in Germany do not show practical interest in rune magic. Through the 1970s and 1980s there developed in Germany a sort of dichotomized universalist or semiuniversalist esoteric runology (represented by Karl Spiesberger, Werner Kosbab, and others) and a tribalist–nationalist esoteric runology (represented by the *Armanen*). All of the groups in Germany use the eighteen-rune Futhork.

The runes have always held a special mystique for those interested in the Germanic way. As a general Germanic Renaissance again began to spread (apparently almost spontaneously from around 1970) in Europe and North America, the runes often figured prominently in the imagery and symbolism of the various groups; for example, the ritual of the Discovery of the Runes used by the Odinic Rite in England, or the name of the journal published by the Ásatrú Free Assembly, *The Runestone*, with its runic masthead. However, no in-depth esoteric runology was undertaken in the early years by any of these organizations.

In the summer of 1974 I came across the book *Runenmagie* by K. Spiesberger[1] in a university library. This occurred after I had received a flash of illumination that consisted of one "audible" word, *RUNA*, just a few days before. From that day forward I worked in the runes. My studies in magic, after having begun well in daimonic splendor, had taken a philosophically uninspiring turn into the morass of Neo-Kabbalism. The runes, and the Way of Woden that is shown through their might, were to set me back on the road to that great power. At the time I was ignorant of the Germanic revival and remained so until 1978. By the summer following the discovery of Spiesberger's book, after I had worked intensively with the philosophy and practice of the *Armanen*-Futhork, I produced a text of my own that was largely a compilation of material from concepts contained in the books of such authorities as K. Spiesberger, Guido von List, and R. J. Gorsleben. This is the unpublished *Runic Magic of the Armanen* finished in August of 1975. This esoteric activity simultaneously led me to a deep academic interest in Germanic religion and magic. By the next year I was a graduate student learning Old Norse and investigating the Way of Woden on an intellectual level as well.

---

[1] Karl Spiesberger, *Runenmagie* (Berlin: R. Schikowski, 1955).

This interest in things Germanic had not begun overnight in 1974, however. The year before, the book *The Spear of Destiny*[2] had sparked my imagination. It also fired my investigative zeal, and I set out to find the original texts on which its edifice was built. Later I found that many had been misused. Still earlier, the words "The ravens of night have flown forth . . ." had rung in my mind as well.

I continued to develop my hidden path in solitude until the summer of 1978, when I made contact with the Ásatrú Free Assembly and began a period of close cooperation with Neo-Germanic groups. At the same time I was completing work on the restoration of the esoteric system of the Elder Futhark of twenty-four runes, which was to result in the text of *Futhark: A Handbook of Rune Magic*.[3] Intellectual studies had led me to the realization that in order to know the runes as they truly are, one must work with the ancient archetypal system as it truly was.

During this same time, but unknown to me, a fellow traveler, David Bragwin James, was working in similar directions in a similar personal situation in New Haven, Connecticut.

It was soon apparent that no group in the English-speaking world was privy to any deep-level runelore, and therefore the burden fell to me to quicken the knowledge of our folk mysteries in a coherent and communicable fashion—no easy task. This work eventually led to the independent formation of the Rune-Gild for the practice and teaching of runework and runecraft. This institution was originally conceived of as an organic part of certain Neo-Germanic religious groups, but this proved quite impossible. It seems the runemasters are a Gild of Outsiders, and as such they remain largely outside other natural, organic structures. It is the purpose of the Rune-Gild to expand the level of knowledge and interest in the genuine Germanic Way and to carry out runework systematically, providing a reliable stream of basic rune skill and rune wisdom to all and giving a way of entry into the Gild Hall to the few.

---

[2] Trevor Ravenscroft, *The Spear of Destiny* (York Beach, ME: Samuel Weiser, 1973.)

[3] Edred Thorsson, *Futhark: A Handbook of Rune Magic* (York Beach, ME: Samuel Weiser, 1984).

6

Historical Rune Magic and Divination

Too many modern rune-magic schools have been forced, either by their ignorance of the timeless traditions or by their inability to gain access to the traditional mysteries, to ignore or to forget the true runic sources handed down to us in lapidary splendor by our ancestors. In this chapter we shall explore the actual runic corpus for evidence of rune magic as it was practiced by the ancients.

The hoary documents carved in stone and metal are but the visible fossils of a living process of runecraft. The literary accounts help us flesh out this process to a great extent, but to understand it one must ultimately plumb the depths of runelore.

Inscriptions

Runic inscriptions represent messages—sendings—of a mysterious nature. They are complex and symbolic communications, which are only sometimes "legible" in the sense of natural language. More often their messages are far more obtuse. However, through a careful analysis of the evidence we may come to some meaningful conclusions on some of the ways rune magic was practiced in days of yore.

As far as operative magical acts are concerned, we can divide the types of runic formulas into seven categories: (1) messages in natural language, (2) symbolic word formulas, (3) futhark formulas, (4) magical formulaic words (e.g., *luwatuwa*), (5) runic ideographs, (e.g., *galdrastafir*), (6) numerical formulas, and (7) the runemaster formulas.

SENDINGS IN NATURAL LANGUAGE

Because the runes enabled them to communicate directly with that *other* (objective) reality, the runemasters could simply write runic messages in natural language to effect some alteration in the environment. These were often magico-poetic vocal formulas symbolically given objective reality through the carving ritual. The most famous of these have been the curse formulas (to prevent the desecration of a grave or holy site) and formulas intended to hold the dead in their graves. "The walking dead," or *aptrgöngumenn*, were a real concern for ancient Northmen. What is sometimes forgotten about this phenomenon is that these corpses often were actually reanimated through the will of some magician and sent to do damage to the community.

In the elder period some of the most noteworthy examples of this kind of magical working are the curse formulas found on the stones of Stentoften and Björketorp in southern Sweden (both from around 650 C.E.). The texts are closely related, so here we will give only the clearer Björketorp example, which reads: *ūtharba-spā! haidR-rūnō ronu falhk hedra, gina-rūnaR. ærgiu hearma-lausR, ūti ær wela-daude sāR that brȳtR.* This formula can be translated: "Prophecy of destruction! A row of bright runes hid I here, magically loaded runes. Through perversity, [and] without rest, on the outside, there is a deceitful death for the one who breaks this [stone monument]." By means of the runemaster's will, and by the power of the runes to communicate that will into objective reality, the legalistic curse formula simply says that whosoever breaks down or disturbs the holy site is cursed unto death by the deceptive power (*wela-*) of the runemaster. (See also the discussion of the Lund talisman on page 40.) Because no judge or executioner is present—and the potential wrongdoer was certainly not literate—the death sentence is carried out purely by magical means. (The stone setting of Björketorp is still intact, by the way.) This triangular arrangement of stones was apparently a ritual and legislative site, as no grave has been found in the area.

WORD FORMULA SENDINGS

Another, more terse form of magical communication was effected by single formulaic words packed with great and multilevel symbolic powers. In the elder period some of these words were *alu* (ale, ecstatic psychic force),[1] *laukaz* (leek),[2] *ehwaz* (horse), *lathu* (invocation), *auja* (good luck), *ota* (terror), and perhaps even *rūno* (rune), secret lore itself.

Many times those words would be inscribed in isolation on various objects in order to invoke the power of the concept the word embodies into the object, or more generally, into the vicinity of the object. Each of the words mentioned above carries with it enormous psycho-magical force and meanings that were very close to the surface for our ancestors but now perhaps lurk in the archetypal depths within us. *Alu* comes from an ancient Indo-European concept of ecstatic power and the magic performed by means of that power. It is undoubtedly related to the Hittite term *alwanzahh*, "to enchant." This basic meaning was then transferred to the sacred, ecstasy-containing substance of the holy ale used in the sacrificial and magical rites of the Germanic folk. In ancient times *laukaz* was a general term for many plants belonging to the genus *allium* (garlic, onion, leek, etc.). These plants hold great health-giving and preserving powers. Also, the leek is especially known for its fast-growing, straight, green stalk—a magical symbol of increase and growth in force and vitality. The magical power of the "horse" concept in Germanic lore is well known and complex (see the E-rune). As a runic word formula it is a sign of transformative power, a symbol of *the* horse, Sleipnir, and of the vital strength of the horse in the horse/man relationship (: ᛖ:).

Each of the foregoing symbol words has a physical counterpart in the natural world. However, there is also a series of concepts that are more abstract. It might be best to consider *rūno* and *lathu* together. Both may ultimately refer to a *vocal* activity on the part of the magician—that is, the vocally performed incantations (*galdrar*) that were intended to call magical forces into objective reality and that were certainly secret in nature and kept hidden from the noninitiate. The word *lathu* is ultimately related to the English term *to load*, and it can be understood in the dynamistic sense of a loading of magical force into an object, or the "invitation" (see German *Einladung*) of divine beings into the area. As another example of the fact that

---

[1] Edred Thorsson, *Futhark: A Handbook of Rune Magic* (York Beach, ME: Samuel Weiser, 1984): 121–122.

[2] Thorsson, *Futhark: A Handbook of Rune Magic*, 111.

rūno was *not* understood to be synonymous with letters or written characters, we can present the reading of the simple runemaster formula on the Freilaubersheim brooch: *Bōso wraet rūna* (Boso carved the rune [singular]). There are other examples that show that the word *rune* was used collectively to mean "secret lore" or "magical incantation" throughout the elder period. The term *auja* refers to a concept very similar to that of *hailagaz* (holy), as it generally means "to be filled with divine or holy power" and hence the well-being and good fortune derived from that state. The opposite side of magical might is referred to by the rather obscure formula *ota*, which is derived from the archaic form *ōhtan* (awe, fear, dread; related to ON *ægi-* in the name of the magical *ægishjálmr* [the helm of awe]). These terms, formulated in staves and therefore subject to ritual manipulation, are thought to be the magical media through which linkage was made between the complex subjective reality of the runemaster and his gild and the objective reality, thereby bringing about conditions in accordance with the will of the "master of the mysteries."

FUTHARK FORMULAS

One of the most conspicuous types of rune-magic formulas is that of the complete or abbreviated futhark (see the examples from the elder tradition in chapter 1). Such inscriptions also were common in the Viking Age and especially in the Middle Ages. In some rare cases it may be that the futhark was carved for teaching purposes, or merely "for practice." However, this certainly could have been more readily accomplished in other, less time-consuming ways. But for the most part the futhark appears to have had a *magical* function. The symbolism of the rune row is at least twofold: (1) it is the collection of all *essential things*, and (2) it is in a special, set *order*. It is the symbol of the order of essential things. Bringing order (cosmic, natural, or psychic) to a given environment (subjective or objective) is certainly a common enough motive for the performance of magic.

RUNE FORMULAS AND MAGICAL FORMULAIC WORDS

If the futhark formula is a symbol of order, then the so-called nonsense inscriptions are symbols of disorder, or of a non-natural order of some kind. We call rune formulas those sequences of staves that seem random and unpronounceable or repetitive. Examples of this kind of formula are especially plentiful on bracteates. There are also those sequences that are pronounceable but that form no known word in the Germanic vocabulary of natural language. These "words" may indeed be from the "language of the gods," a non-natural language received directly from another world. Famous examples of such words are, *luwatuwa, suhura-susi, anoana, salusa-lu, foslau,* and later *suf-fus.* Some may be "decoded," some not. These are but the few remnants of a non-natural, magical language shared by Ódhinn and his earthly Erulians—a language to which access must again be won. Such words were probably first received and spoken by magicians (*seidh-menn*) in trance states and subsequently passed on in the tradition as a part of the vocabulary of magic. Their use in runic formulas is again understandable in terms of the "objectifying principle" of the runes.

IDEOGRAPHIC RUNES

In theory the only kind of character that could qualify as an ideographic rune is a stave of the futhark that stands for its name (i.e., a logograph) or for a word within its field according to scaldcraft. However, there are also certain types of *galdrastafir* (magical signs) that were originally made up of bind runes (staves superimposed one on another) and often highly stylized. We have already met with examples of these on the Sievern bracteate, the Pietroassa ring, the Gummarp stone, and the amulet of Kvinneby. These ideographic runes actually represent a kind of alternate encoding of secret meanings to conceal them further. But the motive for this concealment, this *hiding*, was not to make the text more difficult for other humans to read— few inscriptions, especially the elder ones, were ever meant to be "read" at all. Quite to the contrary, it was intended to make the text more pleasing to and more empathetic with the hidden realms. The more meaning that could be concealed in a terse manner, the more powerfully empathetic the magical message of the runemaster was for the objective, but hidden, other reality of the eight outer worlds.

NUMBER FORMULAS

The topic of runic numerology will be addressed in great detail in chapter 11. At present, let it suffice to say that numerical patterning is another form of concealment, with the same motive as other forms of "magical hiding" in the Germanic tradition.

RUNEMASTER FORMULAS

Any nonmagical interpretation of the many runemaster formulas seems absurd. It is clear that when the runemaster carved the staves of the formula *ek erilaz fāhidō rūnō* (I the Erulian [= runemaster] colored the rune) he was not merely performing some elaborate form of grafitti (although certain psychological processes may be common to both acts). Runemaster formulas represent documents of transformative magical acts in which the rune magician assumed his divine aspect for the performance of some working. It is quite possible that with runemaster inscriptions we are dealing with the remains of but one fraction of a more elaborate ritual process. A runemaster formula could give force to a rite working together with the formula, or it could be the whole of an operant working in itself. In the latter case one will usually find that the runemaster designates himself with various magical names (which are often very similar to some of the holy names of Óðhinn). One of the most famous examples of this is provided by the Järsberg stone in central Sweden. It reads: *ek erilaz rūnōz wrītu. Ūbaz haite, Hrabanaz haite*, "I the Erulian carve the runes. I am called the Malicious-one (= *Ūbaz*), I am called the Raven." This stone, not attached to any grave and probably originally part of a ritual stone arrangement, is then charged by the force of the runemaster in this threatening aspect of "the malicious one" and "the raven." Through the linkage of these foreboding aspects with the site, he is able both to fill it with magical force and protect it from desecrators.

Literature

Without the written sources, especially in Old Norse and Latin, we would have a difficult time scientifically determining the nature of historical rune magic as practiced from about 100 C.E. onward. These accounts, and certain words used in them, give us a key to the structure of runic ritual and provide contexts for certain types of magical acts with runes. There are, however, limits to this evidence. First of all, the texts in question begin to be common only in the Middle Ages, and although they surely represent much older material and reflect archaic practices, we should be aware of this time discrepancy. Second, the saga accounts are, after all, integrated into narrative tales and may have some degree of literary convention built into them. But both of these points are minor when viewed in the broad scope of the tradition. Rune-magic acts apparently were common enough in the Viking and Middle Ages that they form natural parts of the sagas, and they are presented in what might be for some a surprisingly matter-of-fact way.

RUNECASTING

There are no clear examples of runestaves carved for divinatory purposes, but this is no doubt due to the fact that they were scratched on perishable materials. Also, they were perhaps ritually destroyed after use as a matter of normal procedure. It is another odd fact that there is no direct, nonmythological reference to the act of runecasting in Old Norse literature. Despite all of this, which is chiefly based on indirect linguistic evidence and parallel accounts in historical texts, we can be fairly certain that the practice was known.

Linguistic evidence is of two kinds: words for the tools of runecasting and terms that originally must have been characterizations of the results of runecastings.

Actual pieces of wood on which individual runes or runic combinations were carved (and usually colored with blood or red dye) were known in Old Norse as *hlaut-teinar* (sg., *hlaut-teinn*; lot twig) (also known by Snorri Struluson as blood twigs), and *hlaut-vidhar* (lot woods). The original use of the Germanic term *stabaz* (stave, stick) perhaps had to do with the fact that runes were carved on pieces of wood that were most probably used in divinatory practices. The terms *rūno* and *stabaz* were so intertwined by this practice that the words became synonymous. An interesting piece of corroborating evidence is found in the Old English word *wyrd-stæf* (stave of wyrd or weird)—an obvious reference to divinatory use.

Old Germanic dialects are full of compound words that refer to various types of runes/staves. Some are technical descriptions (ON *málrúnar* [speech runes], ON *blódhgar rúnar [bloody runes]*, Old High German *leod-rūna* [song rune], etc.); whereas others give an indication of the reason for which they are to be worked (ON *brim-rúnar* [sea runes—to calm it], *bjarg-rúnar* [birth runes—to help in it], etc.). However, among these there are some designations that seem to classify the results of a runecasting. Some are auspicious (ON *líkn-stafir* [health staves], ON *gaman-rúnar* [joy runes], ON *audh-stafir* [staves of riches], ON *sig-rúnar* [victory runes]); whereas others seem inauspicious (ON *myrkir stafir* [dark staves]; ON *böl-stafir* [evil staves]; OE *beadu-rūn* conflict rune]; ON *flærdh-stafir* [deception staves]). Of course, in many cases the passive readings of these terms could be turned around to active workings.

As far as the actual practice of runecasting is concerned, the best description is provided by Tacitus writing in chapter 10 of the *Germania* (ca. 98 C.E.). Formerly, there might have been a debate as to whether the *notae* (signs) mentioned by him could actually have been runes because the oldest inscription was thought to date from about 150 C.E. But with the discovery of the Meldorf brooch (ca. 50 C.E.), we now have hard evidence that the runes were known from before the time of the *Germania*. The account by Tacitus[3] may be translated:

> To the taking of auspices and drawing of lots they pay as much attention as any one: the way they draw lots is uniform. A branch is cut from a nut-bearing tree and cut into slips: these are designated by certain signs (Latin *notae*) and thrown randomly over a white cloth. Afterwards, the priest of state, if the consultation is a public one, or the father of the family if it is private, offers a prayer to the gods, and while looking up in the sky, takes up three slips, one at a time, and interprets their meaning from the signs carved on them. If the message forbids something, no further inquiry is made on the question that day; but if it allows something, then further confirmation is required through the taking of auspices.

In the *Gallic War*,[4] Caesar, writing in about 55 B.C.E., also mentions "consulting the lots three times" (*ter sortibus consultum*), so this must have been an important aspect of Germanic divination.

Three Eddic passages also give significant magical—and rather cryptic—insight into runic divinatory practices. All occur in mythic contexts. In the "Völuspá," stanza 20: "[the Norns] scored on wood, they laid laws they chose lives, they spoke the "fates" [ON *ørlög*]." In the "Hávamál," stanza 111, there is the instructive passage: "On the chair of the theal [ON *thulr*, cultic speaker], at the well of Wyrd [ON *Urdhr*] . . . of the runes

---

[3] For original text see Rudolf Much, *Die Germania des Tacitus*, 3rd ed. (Heidelberg: Carl Winter, 1967): 189. The translation here is my own. Interested readers may also want to pick up the published translation by H. Mattingly: Cornelius Tacitus, *The Agricola and the Germania* (Middlesex, UK: Penguin, 1970.)

[4] Julius Caesar, *The Conquest of Gaul* (trans. by S. A. Handford) (Harmondsworth, UK: Penguin, 1951): Book I, 53.

I heard it spoken." Earlier in the "Hávamál" (st. 80) man is told that "it is proven when you ask of the runes, which are sprung from the 'divine advisors' [= gods, ON *regin*]."

There are other historical accounts from the viewpoint of Christian observers that tell us little other than that the role of the number three was of great importance.

MAGIC

The runes were of course also widely used for operative magical purposes. A verbal derivative, Old Norse *rýna* (to work magic with runes, or to inquire), shows the close link between illuminative and operative acts. Also, terms that often may seem to indicate the coming to pass of certain events (e.g., *sigrúnar* [victorious outcome]) also can be used to bring about this state through operative action. "Victory runes" are carved and/or spoken to inject objective reality with their power.

At this time perhaps a word should be said about the true and exact meaning of such terms as "victory runes," "ale runes," "birth runes," "sea runes," and the like found in abundance in Old Norse, Old English, and Old High German. Many lay investigators (and some scholars) have generally sought to identify such terms with specific rune*staves* for example, victory runes: ↑↑: and/or :ᚼᚼ:, the former based on the famous Eddic passage in the "Sigrdrífumál," stanza 7 (where Sigurdhr is told to "call twice on Týr for victory"), and the latter on the "skaldic link" between Old Norse *sig* (victory; or modern German *Sieg* for that matter)—and the S-rune. Both suppositions have some merit, and their appeal is not to be denied. However, they do not delve deeply enough into the complex lore surrounding the word *rune* to be able to explain the ways these terms were used. If we always keep it in mind that the old Germanic word *rūno* primarily means mystery and that it is derived from a vocal concept (whisper, roar, etc.), the possible breadth of such terms becomes clearer. *Sig-rúnar* are not *only* runestaves that either signify or bring about victory but also the *galdrar*, or whole poetic stanzas, that work to the same ends. From this developed the use of these terms to indicate normal speech that might have the same effects; for example, Old Norse *gaman-rúnar* (joy runes) became an expression for merry talk, and Old Norse *flærdh-stafir* (deception staves) became a way of saying seductive words. That into late times the ideas of *rún* (rune), *stæf* (stave), and *galdr* (incantation) were sometimes virtually synonymous is shown by the Old

Norse pairs of compounds *líkn-stafir* (healing stave), *líkn-galdr* (healing spell), and *val-rúnar* (death runes)/*val-galdr* (death dirge).

Actual runic carving rituals are depicted several times in Old Norse texts. The saga accounts have the advantage of showing us how the runes were used by magicians in everyday situations, and some cryptic Eddic passages give clear indications of the mytho-magical patterns on which these rites were based.

The "Hávamál," stanza 142, provides a representation of the process of a runic risting (carving) rite as archetypally performed by the Great Runemaster, Ódhinn:

> Runes wilt thou find
> and read the staves,
> very strong staves,
> very stout staves,
> that Fimbulthulr [= Ódhinn] colored
> and made by the mighty gods
> and risted by the god Hroptr [= Ódhinn]

The greatest account of a human runemaster which has survived is that of Egill Skallagrímsson (*Egil's Saga*). Once Egill detects poison in his drinking horn (chapter 44):

> Egill drew out his knife and stabbed the palm of his hand, then
> he took the horn, carved runes on it and rubbed blood on them.
> He said:
>
> > I carve a rune [sg.!] on the horn
> > I redden the spell in blood
> > these words I choose for your ears. . . .
>
> The horn burst asunder, and the drink went down into the
> straw.

Later in the same saga (chapter 72) Egill heals a girl of sickness caused by ill-wrought runes. The *laun-stafir* (secret staves, i.e., coded runes) were carved by a peasant boy trying to cure her, but it only made her sickness worse. The whalebone on which the characters were carved was found lying in the bed!

Egill read them and then he whittled the runes off and scraped
them down into the fire and burned the whale bone and had all the
bedclothes that she had thrown to the winds. Then Egill said:

"A man should not carve runes
unless he knows well how to read:
it befalls many a man
who are led astray by a dark stave;
I saw whittled on the whalebone
ten secret staves carved,
that have given the slender girl
her grinding pain so long."

Egill carved runes and laid them underneath the pillow of the
bed, where she was resting; it seemed to her that she was well
again. . . .

The possible nature and identity of the *laun-stafir* are discussed in chapter 7.
One of the most remarkable uses of runes is in the preparation of the
níðhstöng (cursing pole). Details on its preparation are given in at least two
sagas. Again *Egil's Saga* (chapter 57) gives one example:

. . .Egill [came] up onto the island. He picked up a hazel pole [ON
stöng] in his hand and went to a certain rock cliff that faced in
toward the land; then he took a horse head and set it up on the pole.
Then he performed an incantation [ON *formáli*] and said: "Here I
set up the niding-pole, and I direct this insulting curse [ON *níðh*]
against king Eiríkr [Bloodax] and Gunnhild the queen"—then he
turned the horse head in toward the land—"I turn this insulting
curse to those land-spirits [ON *land-vættir*] that inhabit this land
so that all of them go astray, they will not figure nor find their
abode until they drive king Eiríkr and Gunnhildr from the land."
Then he shoved the pole down into a rock crevice and let it stand
there; he also turned the horse head toward the land and then he
carved runes on the pole, and they said all the incantation [*formáli*].

This may be compared to the description of the *níðhstöng* given in the
Vatnsdœla Saga (chapter 34):

The brothers waited until three o'clock in the afternoon, and when it had come to that time, then Jökull and Faxa-Brandr went to Finnbogi's sheep stall, which was there beside the fence, and they took a pole [ON *súl*] and carried it down below the fence. There were also horses that had come for protection from the storm. Jökull carved a man's head on the end of the pole and carved runes in the pole with all those incantations [*formáli*] that had been said before. Then Jökull killed a mare and they opened it up at the breast and put in on the pole, and they had it turn homeward toward Borg. . . .

Another famous account the rune magic is found in the *Grettir's Saga* (chapter 79) where we read:

[Thuridhr] hobbled . . . as if guided to a spot where there lay a large stump of a tree as big as a man could carry on his shoulder. She looked at it and asked them to turn it over in front of her. The other side looked as if it had been burned and smoothed. She had a small flat surface whittled on its smooth side; then she took her knife and carved runes on the root and reddened them in her blood, and spoke spells over it. She went backwards and widdershins around the wood and spoke very powerful utterances over it. Then she had them push the wood out into the sea, and said it is to go to Drangey and Grettir should suffer harm from it.

One clear example of rune magic performed by a god is also present in the *Poetic Edda* ("Skírnismál," or "För Skírnis," st. 36):

A *thurs*-rune I for thee,
and three of them I scratch
lechery, and loathing, and lust;
off I shall scratch them
as on I did scratch them
if of none there be need.

Here, of course, the divine messenger of Freyr, Skírnir (the Shining-one), is threatening Gerdhr the etin-wife with a curse if she will not agree to become a bride of his lord. This whole poem has many Ódhinic elements in it; for example, the viewing of the worlds from *Hlidhskjálfr*, Ódhinn's high seat, by Freyr and the traversing of the worlds on a horse by Skírnir. Certain interrelationships between Freyr and Ódhinn are explored in chapter 13.

From the historical examples given thus far it is clear that runes could be used to heal as well as to harm. But aside from the mysterious and shamanistic initiatory ritual, were there any other forms of wisdom magic or rituals for self-transformation? The answer is yes. But because of the natural preoccupation with *conflict* in the sagas—they are, after all, stories intended as much to entertain as to recount "historical" events—such rituals are rarely mentioned. When looking at this question, one must remember that the primary purpose of illuminative runecasting was such a transformational process. The runecaster is literally in-*formed* by the communication and is not merely a passive and objectified receiver. That is why true runecasting should not be treated as a profane "game" or done casually by noninitiates. The most remarkable runic ritual of wisdom working is found in the "Sigr-drífumál," which after recounting the twenty-four mythic locations for runes to be carved (sts. 15–17), gives us this invaluable formula in stanza 18:

All [the runes] were scraped off,
that were scratched on,
and blended into the holy mead,
and sent out upon wide ways.

This gives the actual ritual formula for the draught of wisdom, which can be performed imitatively or symbolically.

Although we could wish for more details and examples of the perform-ance of rune workings in the old Germanic literatures, we must take heart in the fact that so much exact information has been left in the fragments we do have. There is enough to enable us to reconstruct with great historical accuracy the physical circumstances of operative rune workings and to some extent illuminative (divinatory) ones.

The operative formula was a threefold process of (1) *carving* the staves, (2) *coloring* them (with blood or dye), and (3) *speaking* the vocal *formáli* that accompanies the graphic forms. This latter step may take many forms, for example, the intoning of rune names, words of power related to the working, the actual words represented by the inscribed staves, or similar poetic forms. The fourth aspect of the operative process is the *scraping off* of the staves from their material medium in order to destroy or transfer their force. This is the simplest form of the ritual we have in explicit representations. However, that more complex ritual forms were sometimes involved in rune workings is strongly suggested by the "Hávamál," stanza 144:

Knowest thou how to carve [rísta]?
Knowest thou how to read [rádha]?
Knowest thou how to color [fá]?
Knowest thou how to test [freista]?
Knowest thou how to ask [bidhja]?
Knowest thou how to offer [blóta]?
Knowest thou how to send [senda]?
Knowest thou how to sacrifice [sóa]?

The terminology of this stanza is clearly connected to rune workings, but only the first three technical terms are purely runic—to carve, to color, and to read (i.e., to interpret runestaves in divinatory workings). The other five terms are more usually designations for processes in sacrificial rites. In Old Norse, *freista* means to test, to put to the test, or to perform. This testing may be the search for signs or omens to corroborate or confirm the results of illuminative workings common to the practice of Germanic divination. *Bidhja* indicates the mode of correctly requesting divine action or "feedback," and the last three terms refer more directly to the modes of actually *sending* sacrifice to the god(s). All of this leads us to believe that sacrificial rites were sometimes performed as an integral part of a rune working.

As far as the ritual form of runecasting is concerned, the Old Norse texts are rather silent. The Northmen, of course, knew a variety of illuminative techniques, many of which are classed as *seidhr* (shamanic, i.e., trance-inducing rites). Runecasting is more analytical and *galdr*-oriented. Because it is known that runes were in evidence in the Germanies during the first century C.E. and because the account given by Tacitus in chapter 10 of the *Germania* is so detailed and contains elements confirmed by later, more fragmentary descriptions, we can be virtually certain that in that passage we possess an authentic formula for runecasting. The basic structure of the working would have been:

1. Cutting and scoring of staves.
2. Calling on the Norns (or other gods).

3. Casting the staves (onto a white cloth).
4. Calling on the gods.
5. Choosing of (three) staves.
6. Sitting on the theal's chair.
7. Reading of the staves.
8. Confirmation by omens, etc.

Runic Codes

One of the most remarkable aspects of the complex "runic system" (see chapter 9) is the possibility of creating various runic codes. The *ætt* system itself makes this complexity possible. This system essentially consists of dividing the entire futhark into three sections or rows. In the elder period there were three rows of eight, as seen in figure 7.1 on page 88.

It is also known from evidence found in five manuscripts that the Old English Futhorc could be divided into these groups, plus a fourth group of four staves, as shown in figure 7.2. The Old English system clearly shows that the first twenty-four runes in the rows were considered an organized whole to which the extra four (five or more in later times) were "eked out."

There is also the later Norse system of *ætt* divisions. Here things get quite curious. The reduction of the rune row from twenty-four to sixteen made an equal division into three groups impossible. So two rows had five and another had six. The row was initially divided in the manner indicated in figure 7.3 on page 89. However, for the construction of runic codes in the Viking Age, this order was usually altered to that shown in figure 7.4. Such reordering also may have been an archaic practice.

The basic idea behind most runic codes founded on the *ætt* system is a binary number set, one of which represents the number of the *ætt* (in the case

Figure 7.1. Ætt divisions of the Elder Futhark

of the elder system a number between one and three), and the other represents the number of the runestave counted from the left (for the elder period a number between one and eight). A simple example would be 2:8 = :ᛊ: (second *ætt*, eighth stave). There are many methods for representing this binary code; in later times the only bounds seemed to have been those in the imagination of the runemaster. Although it was in the Viking and Middle Ages that the art of runic cryptology seems to have reached its peak, the system was certainly known from the beginning of the tradition. The Vadstena/Motala bracteates are the oldest representations of the Elder Futhark divided into *ættir*, but there are also perhaps as many as six elder inscriptions that seem to have some kind of runic code in them.

The ring of Körlin bears the symbol :ᛇ: along with the inscription :ᚢᛚᚨ:. The latter is clearly a reversed *alu* formula, while the former could be a runic code for 2:1 (i.e., second rune of the first *ætt* = : ᚢ :). The stave as it stands is, however, also a bind rune of A + L. This combined with encoded form renders another *alu* formula. This gold ring dates from 600 C.E.

Figure 7.2. Ætt divisions of the Old English Futhorc

Figure 7.3. Ætt divisions of the Younger Futhark

So any method of graphically representing two numbers could be used to write cryptic runic messages. But of course, the "reader" must be familiar with the *ætt* system and all of its intricacies to be able to interpret the message. Other possible runic codes of this kind in the older period are seen on the stone of Krogsta (ca. 550 C.E.), part of which appears : ᚼᛁᚠᛁᛁᛂ ᛋ :, to be read from right to left as SIAINAZ. This makes no linguistic sense. But if we read the : ᛋ : rune as a code stave for 1:1 = : ↑ : (with reordered *ættir*), then it makes sense as *stainaz* (stone). This identifies the object, or it could be the name of the runemaster.

In the inscriptions, code runes are also rare in the English tradition. We do know of the special *ætt* divisions and one inscription, the stone of Hackness (carved sometime between 700 and 900 C.E.). The formula resulting from its decipherment, however, makes no linguistic sense.

Among the most widely practiced of the dozens of known forms of cryptic runes are the *isruna*, *is*-runes. These are known from a medieval German manuscript written in Latin, called the "*Isruna*-Tract." An example (figure 7.5 on page 90) of this runic code system, which spells out the name Eiríkr, is found on the Swedish stone of Rotbrunna in Uppland.

Figure 7.4. Cryptic reordering of the ætt division of the Younger Futhark

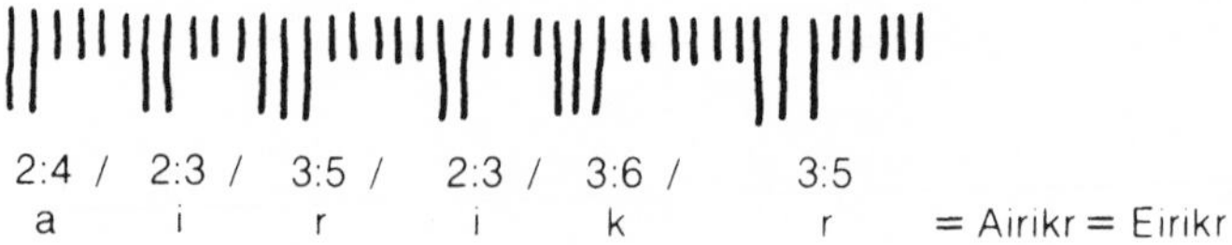

|||ᵘᵘᵘ||⁽ᵘᵘ||||ᵘᵘ|||||ᵞ⁽ᵘᵘ||||ᵞᵘᵘᵘ||||ᵞ|ᵘᵘ|||

2:4 / 2:3 / 3:5 / 2:3 / 3:6 / 3:5
a   i   r   i   k   r   = Airikr = Eirikr

Figure 7.5. Is-runes of Rotbrunna

This latter system may be the key to the passage on rune magic quoted from *Egil's Saga* (chapter 72) on page 81. There Egill speaks of "ten secret staves carved," which were supposed to be scratched in an attempt at a healing working. A good ideographic formula for such a working would be :ᛒᚾ:, *fé* and *úrr*, for energy and vital force. A way of putting these into cryptic, and therefore more magically potent, form in *is*-runes is shown in figure 7.6a. But the unskilled farm boy carved one too many staves, and the resulting formula (figure 7.6b) was hurtful. Figure 7.6b gives *fé* (energy, heat) to *thurs* (gigantic, destructive force)—a formula inappropriate for a healing rite, to say the least. Note also the traditional effect of the TH-rune on women alluded to in the Old Norwegian Rune Poem and Old Icelandic Rune Rhyme! By carving one too many staves in this cryptic formula, the uninitiated rune carver caused the opposite of the willed effect: *Skal-at madhr rúnar rísta, nema rádha vel kunni. . . .*

Besides the *ætt*-based cryptograms, there are a variety of ways to conceal the natural language message of a runic formula. Phonetic values could be shifted along the futhark order, so that ᚾ: = F, : ᚦ : = U, : ᚠ : = TH, and so on. Single runes could be used logcgraphically for their names; for example, in the *Poetic Edda* the stave : ᛘ : is sometimes written as a substitute for ON *madhr* (man). Single key words also can be abbreviated in

3:1 / 3:2   3:1 / 3:3
f   u   f   th

Figure 7.6: a) reconstructed healing formula in is-runes (a total of nine staves); b) farm boy's is-rune formula (a total of ten staves)

various ways. When a single rune stands for a word other than the rune name, we get a glimpse of the hidden lore of the esoteric system of alternate rune names, a subject of ongoing research in the Rune-Gild.

Other common ways to obscure or alter the natural language message are (1) leaving out certain runes (e.g., all of the vowels), (2) scrambling individual words, (3) inscribing the whole text, or just parts of it, from right to left (although this is sometimes so common that it seems to be a regular option), (4) substitution of special nonrunic signs for certain staves, and (5) use of elder runes in younger inscriptions.

The magical (operative) effect of these runic codes is clear. They were not meant (originally, at least) to confuse human "readers." They were intended *to hide the runes*, and what is hidden has effect in the hidden, subjective realms. Thus, an operative link is made between the subjective and objective realities, within the god-sprung framework of the lore of the runes.

Rune Poems

Besides the primary lore of the rune names, shapes, order, and *ætt* divisions, the oldest systematic lore attached to the staves is embodied in the rune poems. There originally were perhaps several of these poems in the tradition, but there can be little doubt that they all belonged to the same sacred body of lore. In this chapter we will present the three major rune poems, along with a little-studied piece of apparent doggerel that may teach us something. All of the poems are translated with a minimum of commentary or internal interpretation. In addition to the rune poems proper—which are essentially series of explanatory poetic stanzas, each beginning with the rune name/stave of a rune row—there are a number of stanzas in the *Poetic Edda* directly relevant to runelore, and we will provide some esoteric commentary on the significance of these sections of the *Edda*. The original purpose of these works may have been to help the runemasters hold certain key concepts in mind while performing runecastings, or they may have just been traditional formulations of the general lore of the runes.

The Old English Rune Poem

"The Old English Rune Poem" records stanzas for the twenty-nine-stave Old English Futhorc. This is especially valuable because it is a source for the lore of the staves of the Elder Futhark not present in the younger row.

The drawback is that some of its stanzas seem to have been altered for a Christian audience. But it is wise to remember that the "Christianity" of the English court society of the early Middle Ages was hardly an orthodox one, and it certainly preserved much of the old heathen culture.

For the text of this poem we are dependent on a transcription made by Humfrey Wanley that was subsequently printed in the *Thesaurus* of George Hickes in 1705. The manuscript of the poem was destroyed in the fire that ravaged the Cottonian library in 1731. Although the manuscript from which the transcription was taken dated from around the end of the tenth century, it is probable that the original version of the poem dates from as early as the late eighth or early ninth century:

ᚠ [Money] is a comfort
to everybody
although every man ought
to deal it out freely
if he wants to get approval
from the lord.

ᚢ [Aurochs] is fearless
and greatly horned
a very fierce beast,
it fights with its horns,
a famous roamer of the moor
it is a courageous animal.

ᚦ [Thorn] is very sharp;
for every thane
who grasps it; it is harmful,
and exceedingly cruel
to every man
who lies upon them.

ᚩ [God/Mouth] is the chieftain
of all speech,
the mainstay of wisdom
and a comfort to the wise ones,

for every noble warrior
hope and happiness.

ᚱ [Riding] is in the hall
to every warrior
easy, but very hard
for the one who sits up
on a powerful horse
over miles of road.

ᚺ [Torch] is to every living person
known by its fire,
it is clear and bright
it usually burns
when the athlings
rest inside the hall.

ᚷ [Gift] is for every man
a pride and praise,
help and worthiness;
and of every homeless adventurer
it is the estate and substance
for those who have nothing else.

ᚹ [Joy] is had
by the one who knows few troubles
pains and sorrows,
and to him who himself has
power and blessedness,
and a good enough house.

ᚻ [Hail] is the whitest of grains,
it comes from high in heaven
showers of wind hurl it,
then it turns to water.

ᛏ [Need] is constricting on the chest
although to the children of men it often becomes
a help and salvation nevertheless,
if they heed it in time.

ᛁ [Ice] is very cold
and exceedingly slippery;
it glistens, clear as glass,
very much like gems,
a floor made of frost
is fair to see.

ᛐ [Harvest] is the hope of men,
when god lets,
holy king of heaven,
the earth gives
her bright fruits
to the noble ones and the needy.

ᛄ [Yew] is on the outside
a rough tree
and hard, firm in the earth,
keeper of the fire,
supported by roots,
[it is a] joy on the estate.

ᛈ [Lot box] is always
play and laughter
among bold men,
where the warriors sit
in the beer hall,
happily together.

ᛉ [Elk's] sedge has its home
most often in the fen,
it waxes in the water

and grimly wounds
and reddens ["burns"] with blood
any man
who, in any way,
tries to grasp it.

ᛋ [Sun] is by seamen
always hoped for
when they fare far away
over the fishes' bath
until the brine-stallion
they bring to land.

ᛏ [Tir] is a star,
it keeps faith well
with athlings,
always on its course
over the mists of night
it never fails.

ᛒ [Birch] is without fruit
but just the same it bears
limbs without fertile seed;
it has beautiful branches,
high on its crown
it is finely covered,
loaded with leaves,
touching the sky.

ᛗ [Horse] is, in front of the earls
the joy of athlings,
a charger proud on its hooves;
when concerning it, heroes—
wealthy men—on warhorses
exchange speech,
and it is always a comfort
to the restless.

ᛗ [Man] is in his mirth
dear to his kinsman;
although each shall
depart from the other;
for the lord wants to commit,
by his decree,
that frail flesh
to the earth.

ᛚ [Water] is to people
seemingly unending
if they should venture out
on an unsteady ship
and the sea waves
frighten them very much,
and the brine-stallion
does not heed its bridle.

ᛝ [Ing] was first,
among the East-Danes,
seen by men
until he again eastward [or "back"]
went over the wave;
the wain followed on;
this is what the warriors
called the hero.

ᛞ [Day] is the lord's messenger,
dear to men,
the ruler's famous light;
[it is] mirth and hope
to rich and poor
[and] is useful for all.

ᛟ [Estate] is very dear
to every man,
if he can enjoy what is right
and according to custom
in his dwelling,
most often in prosperity.

ᚾ [Oak] is on the earth
for the children of men
the nourishment of meat;
it often fares
over the gannet's bath [= sea]:
The sea finds out
whether the oak keeps
noble troth.

ᚫ [Ash] is very tall,
[and] very dear to men
firm on its base
it holds its place rightly
although it is attacked
by many men.

ᛇ [Yew bow] is for athlings
and noble alike
a joy and sign of worth,
it is excellent on a horse,
steadfast on an expedition—
[it is] a piece of war-gear.

ᛄ [Serpent] is a river fish
although it always takes
food on land,
it has a fair abode
surrounded by water,
where it lives in joy.

ᛡ [Grave] is hateful
to every noble
when steadily
the flesh begins—
the corpse—to become cold
to choose the earth
palely as a bedmate;
fruits fall
joys pass away,
bonds of faith dissolve.

The Old Norwegian Rune Rhyme

"The Old Norwegian Rune Rhyme" dates from between the end of the twelfth century and the beginning of the thirteenth. It is clearly part of the same tradition as "The Icelandic Rune Poem," although it is contaminated by some Christian elements. The structure of each stanza is compact and actually twofold: a half-line with two alliterating staves, followed by a half-line containing a single alliterative stave. In the original the two half-lines rhyme. The ideological content of the two half-lines is *seemingly* unrelated; however, the second is actually an esoteric comment on an aspect of the first, which is emphasized in the whole. These stanzas, in an illuminative sense, work much like Zen *koans*:

ᚠ [Money] causes strife among kinsmen;
the wolf grows up in the woods.

ᚾ [Slag] is from bad iron;
oft runs the reindeer on the hard snow.

ᚦ [Thurs] causes the sickness of women;
few are cheerful from misfortune.

ᚬ [Estuary] is the way of most journeys;
but the sheath is [that for] swords.

ᚱ [Riding], it is said, is the worst for horses;
Reginn forged the best sword.

ᚢ [Sore] is the curse of children;
grief makes a man pale.

ᚼ [Hail] is the coldest of grains;
Christ* shaped the world in ancient times

ᚾ [Need] makes for a difficult situation;
the naked freeze in the frost.

ᛁ [Ice], we call the broad bridge;
the blind need to be led.

---

*Originally, *Hroptr* (the Hidden One [= Ódhinn]). The combination *hr* was pronounced "kr" in ON; thus, the alliteration is preserved.

ᛃ [Good harvest] is the profit of men;
   I say that Fródhi was generous.

ᛋ [Sun] is the light of the lands;
   I bow to the holiness.

ᛏ [Týr] is the one-handed among the Æsir;
   the smith has to blow often.

ᛒ [Birch twig] is the limb greenest with leaves;
   Loki brought the luck of deceit.

ᛉ [Man] is the increase of dust;
   mighty is the talon-span of the hawk.

ᛚ [Water] is [that] which falls from the mountain;
   as a force; but gold [objects] are costly things.

ᛇ [Yew] is the greenest wood in the winter;
   there is usually, when it burns, singeing [i.e., it makes a hot fire].

The Old Icelandic Rune Poem

"The Old Icelandic Rune Poem" dates from as late as the fifteenth century but preserves lore from a much older time, as do all the rune poems. The rhyme gives a complex body of information about each alliterating half-line, followed by an independent internally alliterating single half-line, all of which is followed by two words: 1) a Latin "translation" of the rune name, which is often an esoteric commentary, and 2) an alliterating Old Norse word for "chieftain," which also acts as a further key to deeper meaning. Here the Old Norse word is "etymologically" translated into English:

ᚠ [Money] is the [cause of] strife among kinsmen,
   and the fire of the flood-tide,
   and the path of the serpent.
   gold   *"leader of the war-band"*

ᚢ [Drizzle] is the weeping of clouds,
   and the diminisher of the rim of ice,

and [an object for] the herdsman's hate.
shadow [should read *imber*, shower?]   *"leader"*

þ   [Thurs] is the torment of women,
    and the dweller in the rocks,
    and the husband of Vardh-rúna [a giantess?]
Saturn   *"ruler of the* thing*"*

ᚠ   [Ase = Óðhinn] is the olden-father,
    and Ásgardhr's chieftain,
    and the leader of Valhöll.
Jupiter   *"point-leader"*

ᚱ   [Riding] is a blessed sitting,
    and a swift journey,
    and the toil of the horse.
journey   *"worthy man"*

ᚣ   [Sore] is the bale of children,
    and a scourge,
    and the house of rotten flesh.
whip   *"king"* = *descendant of good kin*

ᚼ   [Hail] is a cold grain,
    and a shower of sleet,
    and the sickness [destroyer] of snakes.
hail   *"battle-leader"*

ᚾ   [Need] is the grief of the bondmaid,
    and a hard condition to be in,
    and toilsome work.
trouble   ON níflungr, *"descendant of the dead?"*

ᛁ   [Ice] is the rind of the river,
    and the roof of the waves,
    and a danger for fey men.
ice   *"one who wears the boar-helm"*

ᛅ   [Good harvest] is the profit of all men,
    and a good summer,

and a ripened field.
year   *"all-ruler"*

ᚼ [Sun] is the shield of the clouds,
   and a shining glory,
   and the life-long sorrow [= destroyer] of ice.
wheel   *"descendant of the victorious one"*

ᛏ [Týr] is the one-handed god,
   and the leavings of the wolf,
   and the ruler of the temple.
Mars   *"director"*

ᛒ [Birch twig] is a leafy limb,
   and a little tree,
   and a youthful wood.
silver fir   *"protector"*

ᛘ [Man] is the joy of man,
   and the increase of dust,
   and the adornment of ships.
human   *"generous one"*

ᛚ [Wetness] is churning water,
   and a wide kettle,
   and the land of fish.
lake   *"praise-worthy one"*

ᛦ [Yew] is a strung bow,
   and brittle iron,
   and Farbauti [= a giant] of the arrow
bow, rainbow   *"descendant of Yngvi"*

The *Abecedarium Nordmanicum*

Because the *Abecedarium Nordmanicum* is such a curious piece and is usually not treated in texts on rune poems, we will give it some special attention here. The poem is found in a St. Gall (Switzerland) manuscript, the oldest manuscript of any rune poem, dating from the early 800s. However, its contents do not seem to belong to an ancient heathen tradition. It is written in a mixture of High and Low German, with some Norse characteristics. The manuscript probably was put together by Walafrid Strabo, who studied under Hrabanus Maurus in Fulda from 827 to 829. Hrabanus, who was in turn the student of the Saxon Alcuin, was the greatest single collector of runelore in the Middle Ages. Although all three men were Christian clerics, and their rationale for collecting this material might have been intelligence gathering for missionary work among Ásatrú Norsemen, they inadvertently gathered a great deal of genuine lore of Germanic troth.

ᚠ   fee first,

ᚢ   aurochs after,

ᚦ   thurs the third stave,

ᚨ   the Ase is above him,

ᚱ   wheel is written last,

ᚲ   then cleaves cancre:

ᚼ hail has ᛏ need

ᛁ ice, ᛅ year, ᛋ and sun.

ᛏ Tiu, ᛒ birch ᛘ and man in the middle

ᛚ water the bright,

ᛦ yew holds all.

This "poem" represents the younger Norse runes, but it was composed in the social context of those with knowledge of the Old English Futhorc and its traditions. This is clear from the Old English glosses made in the manuscript (not shown). For the most part, and at first glance, it seems that the words of this poem merely serve to knit the rune names together in proper order (as a mnemonic). But in at least four instances the phrases are esoterically meaningful: (1) "the Ase is above him" (= the thurs)—apparently a theological comment; (2) "and man [is] in the middle"—clearly is not a spatial but cosmo-psychological statement—man is in Midhgardhr; (3) "water [is] the bright one"—this is the shining water of life (see reference to gold in the "Old Norwegian Rune Rhyme"); and (4) "the yew holds everything"—the World-Yew contains the essence of the multiverse.

Comments on Runic Stanzas from the *Poetic Edda*

Besides the rune poems above, there are three lays of the *Poetic Edda* directly relevant to the runic tradition. These are, however, different from the futhark poems. The Eddic poems may delineate, in order, a series of *galdrar* clearly attached to runes, but the exact runic formula may remain hidden. Each stanza is not necessarily attached to a *single* runestave, although it is usually illuminating to classify the meanings in futhark order. Some of these stanzas are clearly meant to be teaching tools. The three lays of the *Poetic Edda* in question are the "Rúnatals tháttr Ódhins" (= "Hávam- ál" 138–165), the "Sigrdrífumál," and the "Grógaldr" (= first half of the "Svipdagsmál").

"THE RÚNATALS THÁTTR ÓDHINS"

The "Rúnatals tháttr" is a key document in the Odian tradition. It should be read and studied in detail by all runesters. The lay is essentially made up of three parts: (1) the rune-winning initiation (138–141), (2) the teaching of technical runelore (142–145), and (3) a catalog of eighteen rune-magic songs (146–164). In the first part Ódhinn is initiated (or initiates himself) into the wisdom of the runes by hanging himself in the branches of the World-Tree, Yggdrasill ("the steed of Yggr"[= Ódhinn], or "the yew column") with its nine worlds, where he is "wounded by the spear." This is a typical shamanistic initiatory theme in which the initiate is subjected to some sort of torture or mock execution (in a cosmologically significant context) in order that he might come face to face with death. To hang the victim in a tree and stab him with spears in *the* traditional way of making human sacrifice to Ódhinn, known from early Roman reports to Viking Age saga accounts. Here Ódhinn gives (sacrifices) his Self to himself—''given to

Ódhinn, myself to myself.'' These words contain the great Ódhinic rune of *gebo*, the true nature of Odian Self-sacrifice. The Odian does not give his Self to Ódhinn, but rather he learns the Odian path and gives his Self to himself.

In this process Ódhinn descends into the realm of Hel (Death); and in that twilight between life and death, in the vortex of intensified opposites (: ᛉ :), he receives the flash of runic initiation, in which the runes are shown to him, and he becomes whole with the essence of the universal mysteries. From this realm he returns to the world of consciousness—the worlds of gods and men—in order to communicate these mysteries to the essences of these realms and to certain beings within them. That the substance of these runes is also contained in the poetic mead is emphasized in stanza 140.

This initiatory myth actually describes not a historical "event" but a timeless process in which "inspired consciousness" (*wōdh-an-az*) melds with the "universal mysteries"—not to be controlled by them but to gain mastery over their use. Its technical aspects give a ritual pattern (one among many) for human workings.

In stanza 141 Ódhinn declares the effect of this on consciousness; it causes it *to become*—to evolve, grow and thrive. The last two lines show the complex, transformationally linguistic nature of Ódhinn's work within himself and among the gods and men. In the "moment" of runic initiation he "takes up the runes screaming"—that is, the melding with the universal mysteries is accompanied by a vibratory emanation, the vocalized *sound*. Hence, the primal link of "mystery" and "sound." In this vortex natural language fails to express the essential totality of the experience, but it is from this vortex that magical scaldcraft is born.

The second part of the "Rúnatals tháttr" contains essential technical runelore, in albeit cryptic form. Stanza 142 instructs us first to "find" and "read" the mysteries, that is, master passive knowledge of them. Learn to understand and interpret the great and mighty staves. Then we are to use them actively: to color, fashion, and carve, to do active workings with them. The next stanza, which has already been discussed in detail (page 84), is a list of technical terms, each a skill to be mastered by the would-be runester. This section is concluded with the injunction not to "oversacrifice"—best results are derived from correct proportion. The last two lines frame the whole:

> Thus did Thundr [= Ódhinn] carve
> before the doom of man;
> there he rose up,
> when he came back.

This makes the primordial, nonhistorical nature of the text clear, and tells us that his "falling back" from the World-Tree was truly a *rising up*. The symbolism of this formula alludes to the Ódhinic transformational path, which is an oscillation between extremes, and to the idea that the World-Tree has not only branches but roots through which Ódhinn wends his way. Individual runestaves can be ascribed to each of the stanzas. This illuminates their essence. The rune row in question would be the Younger Futhark of sixteen staves, to which would be added (for esoteric reasons) the old E-rune and G-rune. The magical aim of each verse is usually self-evident: (1) help in removing distress and conflict of all kinds (through "wealth" : ᚠ :); (2) removal of disease, healing (through "vital force" : ᚼ :); (3) dulling of enemies' weapons (through "destructive force" : ᚦ :); (4) removal of bonds and fetters (through "ecstatic magical force" : ᚨ :); (5) deflection of enemy weapons through direct magical gaze (by the magical directing : ᚱ :); (6) reflection of a magical curse to its source (through redirection of energy : ᚲ :); (7) control of wild combustion (fire) (through cold ordering force : ᛉ :); (8) removal of conflict (though willed reversal of the effect of stress factors : ᛦ :); (9) calming of wild seas (through constricting force : ᛁ :); (10) confusion of destructive agents (through overloading of magical stream in willed direction : ᛃ :); (11) protection of warriors (through loading with the shield of "good speed [= luck]" : ᚺ :); (12) learning of the secrets of the dead (through carving of *helrúnar*—raising the dead along the *axis mundi* : ᛏ :); (13) protection of a warrior at birth (by an endowment of invulnerability through magical enclosure : ᛒ :); (14) illustrative wisdom magic for knowledge of gods and other worlds (through calling up of the divine and cosmic heritage in man : ᛦ :); (15) sending of power to the other worlds (through increase in vital power : ᛚ :); (16) erotic love magic of attraction (through filling with powers of lust toward blending with the opposite : ᛣ:); (17) erotic love magic of binding (through the force of combination of paired opposites :ᛗ:); (18) dynamically erotic magic of exchange (through sex magical initiation : ᛇ :).

It is to be noted that the eighteen magical songs seem to be divided into two groups of nine, with the first nine being songs of magical drawing away of energy and the latter nine being songs of magical increase of energy. Thus, is it always in the magical ebb and flow of the bipolar Odhinic world view.

"SIGRDRÍFUMÁL"

As a runic document, the "Sigrdrífumál" is the most complex in Old Norse literature. It is made up of many sections, each a whole but perhaps artificially linked together. There are three sections in the lay in which Sigrdrífa/Brynhildr, the *valkyrja* and "higher self" of Sigurdhr, gives systematic rune-rede to the hero. The first is in stanzas 6 to 14. Here she catalogs various runic genres: stanza 7—*sigrúnar*, victory runes, by which one gains victory; stanzas 8 and 9—*ölrúnar*, ale runes, by which one gains protection through higher consciousness and power; stanza 10—*bjargrúnar*, help-in-birth runes, by which one brings things forth into being; stanza 11—*brimrúnar*, sea runes, by which one calms natural disturbances; stanza 12—*limrúnar*, limb runes, by which one heals sickness; stanza 13—*málrúnar*, speech runes, by which one gains eloquence; and stanza 14—*hugrúnar*, mind runes, by which one gains intelligence.

In the second rune-rede section (sts. 17–19) Sigrdrífa indicates twenty-four things on which Ódhinn "carves runes." The mythological nature of these objects (and the number of them!) shows this to be a working of cosmic shaping through the mysteries of idea–form–vibration on the part of the primal world consciousness—*Wōdh-an-az*. The three stanzas are actually attributed to the Mimir aspect, which communicates primal wisdom (see chapter 13.) The first lesson to be learned from these three stanzas is that twenty-four is the cosmological "key number" of wholeness, and that this whole system is consciously "vivified" by the will of Ódhinn expressed through the runes.

The third section (stanzas 24–39) consists of a list similar to what we met in the "Hávamál" and will find again in the "Grógaldr." But this one is more didactic in the style of the earlier stanzas of the "Hávamál" and less "magical." The number of concepts systematically categorized is eleven (the number of *sól* in the younger row—ethical force).

As a whole, the three runic sections of the "Sigrdrífumál" have the function of imparting to the hero operative magical, cosmological, and ethical wisdom. These are depicted as having their source in the "higher" *fylgja-valkyrja* self.

"GRÓGALDR"

The "Spell of Gróa" is a poem of a type similar to the "Völuspá" in that a dead seeress is summoned from her slumber in Hel to give needful wisdom. The seeress Gróa (from Welsh *groach* [witch]) sings nine magical songs to her son, Svipdagr, who called upon her to give him magical aid in his quest for the etin-wife Menglodh. The magical intent of the nine songs are as follows: (1) to steady one's true will (: ᚠ :); (2) to protect one from malicious spells (: ᚾ :); (3) to provide safe passage through dangerous water, and maintenance of consciousness in the dark realms (: ᚦ :); (4) to give control over enemies' actions (: ᚨ :); (5) to liberate from bonds (: ᚱ :); (6) to still stormy seas (: ᛁ :); (7) to provide the life-heat of fire (: ᛦ :); (8) protection from malicious undead (: ᛃ :); (9) to make conscious link with the creative realm of eloquence (: ᛉ :).

Two things should be noted when reading the catalog stanzas of the "Rúnatals tháttr," "Sigrdrífumál," and "Grógaldr": (1) they do not necessarily follow in the futhark order, and (2) it seems that the magical songs *themselves* are often not overtly recorded (but rather descriptions of their purposes and effects). The keys to these encoded forms are given in Rune-Gild work.

Part Two

Hidden Lore

Inner Runelore

In part 1 we hoped to establish the firm *traditional* basis in exoteric aspects of runelore with insights into hidden and timeless lore. In part 2 we will continue to base ourselves as much as possible in the solid traditional framework. This emphasis that the Gild always places on bases in verifiable tradition (i.e., historical runic systems, old Germanic literatures, ancient histories) is important if we are to avoid being forced to accept one man's (or one group's) "revelation."

But of course, the Gild is an instrument for the practical application of this tradition, so we will go well beyond the limited academic/scientific aspect. We quicken the wooden forms of academic findings with the inspiration of Ódhinn, but we remain forever open to new findings and conclusions reached through purely intellectual means as well. Ideally, the systematic collection of data and the logical analysis of those data to form rational conclusions, the intuitive understanding of the multiversal mysteries and the inspired use of those mysteries to transform or shape reality should work in tandem, each feeding the other. Hidden doors are thereby opened in both directions. This is the work of the Rune-Gild on all its levels.

"Rune" is the "Word of the Gild." It is in and of itself a magical formula. Paradoxically, as a word, the more we refine the definition of *rune*, the broader its meaning becomes. This is why the ambiguous "translation" as "secret" or "mystery" is suitable. (It is perhaps worth repeating that the term *rune* only secondarily refers to the letter forms [staves] commonly called runes.)

As a magical *word, rune* must be understood from self-created viewpoints, and as such its true "meaning" cannot be communicated through profane, natural speech. As a magical word it is "whispered in our ear" by the Ódhinn within.

Starting points on this road are the realizations that on a cosmological level runes are focal points of energy/substance in a complex implicit cosmic framework, and on a "psychological" level they are "points of reference" at which cosmic intelligence interacts with human intelligence. Knowledge of this level concerning the character of the runes must be allowed to go with you in all runic investigations; only so armed will the athling be able to find his way in the complex realms of runelore.

Runelore Tables of the Elder Futhark

The following tables supplement the lore in *Futhark*. If anything, these associations are more traditional (i.e., based on information gleaned from ancient Germanic sources) than the more operative/magical slant of the tables in *Futhark*. The surest way for runesters to expand their own fields of meaning for the runes is to meditate on their shapes, sounds, and names, but most of all on their corresponding rune poem stanza (if any). It must be constantly kept in mind that the lore of each individual runestave is only part of the mystery; the rest is in the hidden ways in which the runes are woven together in a multidimensional web-work of being. Therefore, the lore of these twenty-four tables must be read within the context of sections on the runic system and rune worlds (chapter 10). It is of the utmost importance for true runic understanding that the vitki know not only what makes *fehu fehu* but also how *fehu* is bound to other runes in the system and how hidden lines of connection may be discovered. Each stave is internally suggestive of wider vistas, and each points outward from its center to interconnections with the essences of other runes. The would-be runester's main task with these tables is the acquisition of a basic and instinctual "feel" for the meaning of each rune as a category but a category surrounded by a kind of semipermeable membrane that allows interchange with sympathetic energies and essences but acts as insulation against antipodal concepts.

Here we will especially concentrate on what might be called in our modern language the mythological, cosmological, and psychological aspects of each mystery. Each of the sections can be seen as esoteric commentaries on the relevant rune poem stanzas as well.

fehu
(fee)

Mythologically, the F-rune is bound to the three great deities whose names begin with its sound—Frigg, Freyja, and Freyr. These divinities derive some of their power from the mystery of *fehu*. From the numinous fire of *fehu* Frigg and Freyja receive their gifts as seeresses. From this common source runecasters derive their ability to "read the runes aright" in divinatory work.

Fehu is the mystery of *gold*. That is, it is the numinous power of that which is called money or wealth in our society (which is now dominated by these "pecuniary mysteries"). This rune exists in a great ecological system of power or energy. The rune must be *yielded* into receptive fields—: ◇ :—in order to be increased. It increases in power through circulation, and it is transformed from one shape to another. This must not, however, be done blindly but rather with foresight and wisdom.

The *fehu* power naturally belongs in the hands of the true athlings, and it is their responsibility to see that it is properly used. Those who do not do so face the natural withering process ruled by "the lord" as a representative of the gods. Abrogation of such responsibilities leads to strife.

In the cosmology this is the true outward force of the primal cosmic fire—the expansive force that answers to contraction and solidification in ice (: | :). This is a fire generated out of water and in the dark depths of the multiverse—and in the dark corners of the self.

It is within the self that the power of the *fehu* is most important to the runester. The F-rune is a force that lies hidden in most souls—like a wolf in the woods—yet can be raised along the path of the grave-fish (serpent). From death shall come life; from darkness, light.

uruz
(aurochs)

In the mythology *uruz* is to be identified with the original cosmic bovine Audhumla (see chapter 6). This is the undomesticated "wild" force of formation, the concentrated will-to-form. As such, *uruz* is the mother of manifestation. It is the process of ordering substance (Ymir), which leads to the shaping of the world in its manifold multidimensional form.

Uruz is the most vital of energies. It is a fire blended with the waters of life, a vital fire that can remove all weakness—all the dross (such as Audhumla's tongue!)—and transform the weak into the strong. If, however, this vital energy is spent in the wrong direction, unguided by wisdom, it can become destructive to the individual or to society.

The will-to-form is a powerful deep-seated instinct in man (hence, it is "on the moors")—as is the instinct to *trans*form with which it must work in tandem. Part of the will-to-form is the desire to defend the form, practically at any cost—to defend the security of the "homeland" (: ᛉ :) of the soul.

The horns of the "beast" mentioned in "The Old English Rune Poem" are of extreme importance. Both of them point upward naturally but downward in the runestave. This twofoldness indicates manifestation in the objective universe and the ability to penetrate into other dimensions by the force of will.

thurisaz
(thurs)

The : ᚦ : is the sign of pure action, potency, and instinctual "will" devoid of self-consciousness. It is the embodiment of directed cosmic force in the multiverse as a combination of polar energies projected in a straight line.

This form of raw power is held, on the one hand, by the thurses (giants) and is directed against the consciousness embodied in the Æsir. However, the Æsir are able to combat this power, and match might with might, through their defender, the warder of Ásgardhr—Thórr.

The TH-rune is therefore not only that of the thurses but also of the thunder and its god, Thórr. This is due to their common origins as the result of the clash of polarized forces (see chapter 10) and also shows their common methods and motivations. Each is a *reactive* force. The thurses respond to the expansion of consciousness in the Æsir, and Thórr responds with Mjöllnir to the resistance of the thurses. Thus, a balance is achieved but a precarious balance.

Thurisaz (3) is an assimilation of the potential energy contained in any two polarized extremes and the kinetic expression of them. Through this mystery the TH-rune is also the power of regeneration and fertility. As the thunder heralds the crop-bringing rains, so *thurisaz* breaks down opposition and releases energy so that new beginnings can be made. Here it is closely related to one of its formal correspondences : ᛒ :, but : ᛒ : is the "releaser" and : ◊ : the "container."

This tension is perceived by most individuals as a source of stress, but to the few (athlings or Erulians) it is a source of strength.

The "thorn" is not only a symbol of the phallus but also of the whole psychosexual impulse used by athlings to transform the self.

It is rather clear that on one level the TH-rune is an expression of the combination of the F- and U-runes: fiery energy organized and directed, force and formation combined and directed.

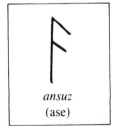

ansuz
(ase)

The A-rune embodies the powers of synthetic, Ódhinic (Odian) consciousness in the multiversal structure and in the psychological complex of humanity. It is the rune of consciousness, especially that which successfully integrates the right and left hemispheres of the brain. This rune is the magico-ancestral power innately transmitted from generation to generation since the dawn of mankind. *Ansuz* is the name for an ancestral sovereign divine being. In the singular this usually refers to Ódhinn as *the* god. This link between the consciousness of the gods and the mind of man remains unbroken. The thurses and their "gods" seek to break it.

The powers contained in : ᚠ : were given (and these are their *only* gifts) by the Ódhinic triad of Ódhinn, Vili, and Vé (or in another version Ódhinn, Hœnir, and Lódhurr) at the shaping of humanity (see chapters 12 and 13). These powers are received by humanity as the agents by which it can transform itself through the quest for knowledge and the expression of that knowledge in word and work, guided by the Ódhinic model.

On a cosmological level *ansuz* describes an ecology of energy. It is the medium through which power is received, the receptacle of that power, and the power itself when *expressed* through the inspired mental state. This is the rune of the magical word and breath, of the synthesis of linguistic thought with nonlinguistic, image forming power in the poetry of the Erulians and skalds.

raidho
(riding)

Raidho is the symbol of the cosmic law of right order-ing in the multiverse, in mankind, and in the soul. It is a mystery the outward face of which we experience each day in the rising and setting of the sun and in the cycles of activity and sleep. All rhythmic action is ascribed to *raidho*—dance, music, and poetic *forms*.

It is by the might of this rune that institutions of all types are organized: states, religious bodies, guilds, and so on. When those natural laws are broken, the power of *raidho* rebalances them—sometimes violently.

The R-rune is the vehicle ("wagon") for and the pathway (the whole "ride") along the journey of *becoming* in the rune worlds. This path is hard and difficult at times—often in hostile social or natural environments—and a strong vehicle (= mental powers) and horse (= spiritual substance; see *ehwaz*) are needed in order to be successful.

This is the path of rightly ordered *action*—ritual working. It is the network of roadways between the worlds and an important part of the equipment needed to traverse these paths.

Raidho rules mathematical (geometrical) proportion, interval, and logical reckoning of all kinds. It is the rune of cognition. This is the might by which tally-lore works—active harmonization of forces appropriate to a willed end.

One of the great mysteries of the R-stave is its relationship to the idea of "wheels" within the psychophysical complex of man (see the Latin gloss *iter* [wheel] in "The Old Icelandic Rune Poem"). It is on these "wheels" that the magical journey of initiation is made.

The flow pattern of force in *raidho* is always directed, but it has a spiraling effect as well, which actually *concentrates* the force to a given aim. Its usefulness as a working tool should not be overlooked.

kenaz
(torch)

This is the rune of creativity—or more accurately, in Germanic terms, of the ability *to shape*. This is symbolized by *controlled fire*—the torch—but also by the fires of the hearth, harrow (= altar), forge, and pyre. Each serves the human will to shape and reshape itself or its environment. In a person this is the bright light that all recognize as "charisma." Although this is ever-present within the runester, it is most awake in "working states," that is, when inspiration is high but physical activity is restive.

Kenaz is the root of all technological knowledge, the rune of the craftsman and the crafty one—Wayland (ON Völundr) and Loki. It is also the mystery of the deep connection between sexuality and creativity that is so characteristic of the Óðhinic path.

The hidden root concept behind *kenaz* is dissolution, whether by organic means (see the Norse rune name *kaun* [ulcer, sore]) or by fire (torch). This dissolution is necessary for reshaping to take place in accordance with a willed plan. In a sense this is the *solve* portion of the alchemical formula *solve et coagula* (dissolve and coagulate). Here : ᛗ : would be the *coagula* portion—the recombination of forces in a transformed, self-aware essence: ᛁᚹᛁ.

In many ways the K-rune is a culmination of the process begun in the A-rune and working through the R-rune: inspiration rationally crafted.

gebo
(gift)

This is the rune that signifies the Gift of Óðhinn in his triadic forms (see chapter 13)—the gifts of consciousness, life-breath, and form.[1] Here the emphasis is on the exchange of power—the flow of force from one system into another to be transformed and returned to its source.

Within human society this is most evident in the economic field—the process of giving and receiving, the object of which is *fehu* and/or *othala*. Such an exchange builds strong bonds within society, and the same process is carried out between gods and

---

[1] Edred Thorsson, *Futhark: A Handbook of Rune Magic* (York Beach, ME: Samuel Weiser, 1984): 76.

men to build strong bridges between the worlds. *Gebo* is the rune of sacri-fice (or "making sacred")—of giving to the gods and their obligatory return gifts to man. This is the mystery of the interdependence of gods and men. The power of this mystery is exhalted and internalized within the runester in the E-rune.

The : X : is the sign of the "magical (or alchemical) marriage." This again finds expression in |X| (*mannaz*), where the process is brought into full manifestation, and in |X| (*dagaz*), where the process is absolutely internal and eternal. The most powerful example of this magical union is found in the *Völsunga Saga* where Sigurdhr, mounted on his otherworldly steed, Grani (see : M :), pierces the ring of flames and ascends the mountain Hindarfjell (Rock of the Hind) to awaken the sleeping *valkyrja*, Sigrdrífa (or Brynhildr). Here we have what is perhaps the most archaic version of the "Sleeping Beauty" tale. On this mountaintop he ritually exchanges vows with her and receives runic wisdom from her. This process describes the attainment of communion with the "higher" or "divine self" of the runester.

The ecstasy of : X : is of a serene type—the quiet balance of perfectly harmonized inner concentration of flowing vital forces.

wunjo
(joy)

The W-rune is the harmonization of elements or beings of common origin (nations, tribes, clans, families) and the magical power to recognize hidden affinities between sympathetic entities. The *wunjo* describes the inner, subjective feeling one attains when in a state of inner/outer harmony—with self and environment. This is an *active* willed harmony toward specific evolutionary goals. The *wunjo* marshals diverse but sympathetic forces and/or beings to a common purpose. This is why it is the mystery that rules the bind-rune-making process.

"The Old English Rune Poem" gives specific guidelines for the winning of such *wunjo*. There we learn that the runester should separate the self from most woe of all kinds (but keep a little), and further have three things: (1) OE *blæd* ("prosperity": the inflow and outflow of energy); (2) *blyss* ("bliss": to be filled with a sense of meaningfulness and joy); and (3) *byrg geniht* ("a good enough enclosure": a good house of the soul). One needs vital breath, a psychological sense of meaningfulness, and a healthy body—

after cleaving away negative influences detrimental to the concentrated work.

Wunjo also comes when the runester is able to make such a blend-work in the objective world—to bind and marshall forces to do his will.

hagalaz
(hailstone)

This is the sign of the primal reunion of cosmic fire and ice—the poles of the multiverse—in the energized, yeasty seed-form: the cosmic hailstone, or "hail-egg," that gives rise to Ymir (see chapter 10).

Hagalaz is the framework of the world, the pattern upon which the multiverse is fitted out by the triadic root of consciousness—Óðhinn-Vili-Vé. The H-rune contains the complete model of absolute potential energy, as it holds the full dynamism of fire and ice in its form. From this harmonious balance of all-potential, an internal evolution can take place within its space.

Numerical symbolism is very important for *hagalaz*. Nine is the number of completion, fruition, and dynamic wholeness in the Germanic system. All of this comes together in : ᚺ : (9). Nine is the number of worlds in the branches and roots of the World-Tree, Yggdrasill, which is the innate pattern present in both the seed and the full grown tree.

The H-rune is the pattern of completion implicit in the seed of every evolving or growing thing. As the whole yew is contained in a hidden genetic code in the berry, so too is the completed, transformed cosmos held in the world-seed. *Hagalaz* is the code—the pattern of becoming and completion. This is the hidden form of perfection toward which all *conscious* shaping (creation) is directed.

The "hailstone" is the rune mother; all runes are held, and can be read, within its form when contained in a solid (see figure 9.1 on page 122). This is ultimately a multidimensional model, also present in the Yggdrasill pattern discussed in Chapter 10, page 154.

Hagalaz is the unification of all opposites into all-potential. Within its mystery is contained the power of transformation, of the evolution from form to form along a consciously or mythically determined pattern.

Hail also has its destructive aspects, which can be turned to the advantage of the runester if they are directed outward in a protective way.

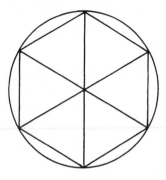

Figure 9.1. Mother rune of the hailstone

nauthiz
(need)

As the rune poems show, the N-rune can be experienced in unpleasant ways by those who do not have the understanding to *use* its power. *Nauthiz* is the force of cosmic resistance to the will and its actions. This is the source of the accumulation of layers of psychic substances that are the essence of what the Norse called *ørlög* (see the P-rune). But this "need" imposed from outside the consciousness can be the source of salvation for the runester who knows how and when to use it (see "The Old English Rune Poem").

The N-rune is resistance to actions, a cosmic friction between substances. This internal stress can be transformed into strength through the mystery of the need-fire (fire made by friction between two inert materials). Once the flame is kindled, the cold of need is alleviated. But without "need" the fire would never have been discovered in the first place. In this rune can be seen the root of the proverb "Necessity is the mother of invention."

As we look deeper into the mystery of the need-fire, we see that it is a self-generated flame. In the realm of consciousness this is to be understood as a certain tension or friction between aspects of the psyche. This leads to the kindling of the flame of higher consciousness that is attainable only through these means.

Because of the absolute necessity for resistance in the cosmos before manifestation can come about, the N-rune is both the mystery of cause and effect and of the Nornir (Norns). The three Norns (see the P-rune) came forth out of Jötunheimr and thereby established the law of cause and effect and its resistance to the will of the Æsir. This brought about the laws of entropy, and thus the seeds of cosmic destruction were sown. Whenever anything is brought forth out of becoming into being, the laws of the Norns and those of the N-rune are activated. This particular law must be kept in mind in all operant forms of runework. It is the rune of "coming forth into being."

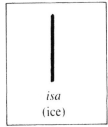

isa
(ice)

The "ice" in the I-rune is not to be identified with that of Niflheimr but rather with the ice stream that flows out of that cold world toward the fire of Muspellsheimr. It is an extension of a concentrated force of absolute contraction or an absolute stillness or lack of vibration. The power of *isa* attracts the fire toward the "center" and makes what we call "matter" possible by formulating the hailstone (: ᚼ :). The I-rune is a kind of *prima materia* (or the force of density that makes such a substance possible). It is the absolute power of inward-turning force that is as destructive as fire (expressed in : ᚠ :), but each balancing the other is the state sought by the conscious forces in the multiverse. When nonconscious forces gain supremacy, the pattern goes out of balance, and the destructive aspects of fire and ice are unleashed. It must be remembered, however, that this ebb and flow is to be expected in an evolving universe. The periodic release of the destructive forces is necessary to real change.

In the individual *isa* makes possible the manifold, polypsychic *omniego* (all-I), that is, ego awareness of all aspects of the whole psychophysical complex (see chapter 12). It holds these aspects together in a harmonious, preset pattern and is most evident when the mind is totally stilled and concentrated. The I-rune acts as a sort of psychic bonding material that can hold the self together through the stressful initiatory process. Unbalanced by the dynamic mysteries, this static bonding material leads to dullness and stupidity.

The : ᛁ : is the mystery of the concentrated point and of its first extension—the line. These two images are used as bridging tools in gaining conscious access to other dimensions outside Midhgardhr. *Isa* is the solid floor on which the consciousness can make transitions, but it is sometimes only as wide as a hair and does not make for an easy journey.

jera
(year)

The J-rune is the sign of the solar year of twelve months; its mystery refers to the "summer" half of the year, when crops are sown, grown, and harvested. (The old Germanic calendar only had *two* seasons, summer and winter. "Spring" and "fall" refer only to short intervals at the borders of these tides.)

The central power of this rune lies in its *cyclical* nature. It is the rune of "eternal return." *Jera* embodies the idea of arising, becoming, and passing away to new beginning present throughout the rune row; and its position as a *core rune* (with : ⌡ :) shows its central importance.

It is the dynamic dyad and the ominpresent circumference.

Jera actually means "the fruitful year," or "the harvest." This is the reward reaped after a cycle of hard work within the natural (and numinous) laws. The symbolism of the agricultural process makes the meaning of *jera* clear. The seeds do not ask who planted them or why, only how they were planted. If the planting has been done *right*, the harvest *should* be good (see : ⌐ :). *Jera* is the reward for right work.

The mystery of the J-stave is fundamentally linked to the first and last staves, as symbols of peace, prosperity, and freedom.

The J-rune is the cosmic millstone, the cosmic axis of which is the EI-rune.

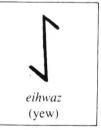

eihwaz
(yew)

The EI-rune is the omnipresent center axis of the cosmos—the *omphallos* of the world—and is the second in the core dyad of the rune row.

This is the vertical axis of the World-Tree, Yggdrasill, the channel along which the cosmic squirrel, Ratatöskr, like an electric arc, spreads discord between the eagle at the summit of the tree and the great serpent, Nidhhöggr, at its roots.

The EI-rune synthesizes extreme opposites—life/death, day/night, summer/winter—in a dynamic way (see the TH- and D-runes and note the numerical correspondences: 3-13-23). This rune penetrates through the three realms: the heavens, middle-earth, and underworld—Ásgardhr/Midhgardhr/Hel. It is the path of transformation of essences in any of these realms into essences of any of the others. "Material" objects can be made "spiritual" by this mystery.

The EI-rune is the latent, self-contained, transformational fire from within (activated by the N-rune and manifest in the K-rune). This is the hidden and immortal fire of the will that *can* remain vital in death (winter)—the hard spirit of perseverance.

It is along the "column of the yew" within the individual that the transformative magical fire is to be generated, rising *and* descending through the "wheels" of the body (see the S-rune). It is to this great mystery that the rune poems refer.

perthro
(lot cup)

This is the most guarded of the runes. It is the cultic symbol of the secret of *ørlög*—the mystery of wyrd. This is the power of the Nornir and one that complements the force of consciousness present in the Æsir. The runester must learn to investigate the way of wyrd that he may understand it and, when need be, overcome it. (This is the great Ódhinic accomplishment at *Ragnarök*.)

The P-rune is a sign of the path of the investigation of *ørlög* through the methods of runecasting. *Perthro* is the cup or framework from which, or into which, the runestaves are cast in divinatory workings. This is a symbol of the Well of Wyrd—the *Urdharbrunnr* (Well of Urdhr, the first and eldest Norn).

In *perthro* we find a synthesis of the laws of cause and effect (x causes y, which sets z in motion) and the laws of synchronicity (x, y, and z occur [significantly] together). Causality is a law of the horizontal (mechanical) plane, synchronicity of the vertical axis of consciousness. The synthetic element is the psychic dimension of time. This force, in conjunction with that of the N-rune and the B-rune, is the principal agent of *change*, or becoming, in the multiverse.

The idea of wyrd (and of *ørlög*) also partakes of this synthesis of horizontal and vertical reality. Wyrd actually means "that which has 'become' or 'turned.'" So it, like *ørlög*, which means "primal layers (of action)," has the mystery of past time bound up with it. This "pastness" is of vital importance in the Germanic way of thinking. Only the "past" and the "present" have any objective reality. The "future" is a mass of undifferentiated all-potential for becoming. It is to be shaped by a combination of forces—cyclical laws, organic streams of life-force and tradition, the patterns of consciousness existing in the gods and other entities, and the will of man (especially that of runesters). Nowhere is this more apparent than in the names of the three great Norns—Urdhr (that which has become), Verdhandi (that which is becoming), and Skuld (that which *should* become). Linguistically, the words *urdhr* (ON) and English wyrd (weird) are identical (the loss of the initial *w* is the result of the same regular rule that turns Wōdhanaz into Ódhinn).

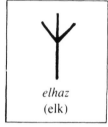

elhaz
(elk)

Elhaz is the divine link between a man and his fetch (see chapter 12). The Z-rune describes the power of attraction between the mind of man and its psychic counterpart, the "divine self." This force of attraction works together with the mystery of *sowilo* to generate the magical will. It is a symbol of the *valkyrja*, the protective aspect of the fetch-wife, which is often magically attached to a sword or other symbolic weapon. (This is the hidden meaning of "The Old English Rune Poem," stanza 15: elk-sedge = sword.) This symbolic link between horn and sword is nowhere more evident than in the myth of Freyr. After surrendering his sword in exchange for the etin-wife Gerdhr, it is said that he had only a horn with which to do battle.

The : Y : also describes the rainbow bridge, Bifröst, again a symbol of the link between Midhgardhr and the realms above and below.

In the Z-rune we see the force of protection that can come only with a linkage with the "personal divinity." This is the entity that the Greeks knew as the *daimon* and the Romans called the *genius*. In runelore the fetch or *valkyrja* is the source of this inspiration as the most direct link between the individual and the ultimate source of inspiration, Ódhinn.

The image of the stave : Y : is one of the most potent in Germanic symbology. It indicates the splayed hand (= protection, humanity), the horns of the solar hart lifted to the heavens in pride and potency, the swan in flight (a reference to the *valkyrja*), and the Germanic arm posture for prayer and invocation. Some of this makes clear why this form was eventually used for the younger "man"-stave.

The loading with magical, numinous, or spiritual force effected through this rune implies a person or place with so much force that it becomes sacred, set apart and protected by divine power.

Also, there is a natural, underlying connection between this rune and the : ʃ :—the yew-stave. This is expressed in many ways; most graphic, however, is the formal relationship. The probable original stave-form was

: ⱬ :, and in time : ⱬ : became the younger yew-stave (which is an alternate form of the elder *elhaz* as well).

sowilo
(sun)

The sun is the guiding beacon on the roads of becoming. It is the light of consciousness—and its pattern, which stands in the objective universe for all of those who seek to transform themselves to see. The archetypal sun, and its counterpart the "night sun" (= the Pleiades), guide the "seafarer" from one zone of consciousness to another, from one "land" to another. This is the goal that gives motivation to the will. In skylore this is "the star" of the elliptic (the Pleiades), which at night travels the same path as the sun does by day.

In ancient Nordic symbolism the sun is seen as a wheel or as a shield. That is, it has transformative and protective, nurturing aspects. As a wheel, *sowilo* is a sign of the wheels along the path of the yew column, Yggdrasill, by which the runester consciously evolves. *Sowilo* is the shield of the consciousness and provides it with greater significance toward which to strive. One who has developed the will by the light of the S-rune (in *all* of its aspects) is blessed with honor and success.

The sun describes a counterbalance to the power of : | :. In the row, however, both are necessary to a stable whole development of the world and of the runester. The S-rune also has been connected with the serpentine mysteries of the north, which involve the centers at which flows of heavenly and chthonic forces converge at a point on the surface of the earth. The power of the : ⟩ : breaks down psychological or cosmic inertia and transforms it into a vital, dynamic force.

tiwaz
(Týr)

The *tiwaz* is also a guiding beacon; but unlike the dynamic circular pathway of the S-rune, the T-rune is a beacon of a much more distant, deep, and serene force—that of the Lodestar, Pole Star, or North Star (Polaris). It is also called "the Star" by the ancient Germanic sailors—the axis star that keeps its troth, and around which all other stars revolve. (See also "the Star" at the circumference of the elliptic in : ⟩ :.) The North Star is a visible symbol of the god-force of *tiwaz* as the summit of the world column—the *Irminsūl*.

The cosmogonic force of Týr is expressed in the initial process necessary to the shaping of the multiverse: the separation or polarization of the cosmic substances that allows for the vital glories of manifestation between the poles of fire and ice. The T-rune describes the aspect of the cosmic column that keeps these separate, holding cosmic order.

This is the essence of the god Týr (English Tiw). (Significant aspects of the T-rune are discussed in chapter 13.) It is the power of detached, transcendent wisdom at the center of things. This contrasts with the wide-ranging multiformed essence of the A-rune.

In the human realm, with this rune the god Týr rules over the *thing* (legal assembly) of the Germanic peoples. He measures out justice in accordance with the *law* (see also *ørlög*, "or-law," in this regard).

The T-stave is a sign of "law and order" in both the cosmos and the world of men.

berkano
(birch)

It is meaningless to attempt to identify the natural tree to which "The Old English Rune Poem" refers under this stave. The B-rune is a numinous reality, not a botanical organism.

Berkano is the great and many-faceted "Birch Goddess," who rules over the process of human and earthly transformations; for example, the critical human rites of passage—birth, adolescence, marriage, and death—and the seasonal round of agricultural year. The B-rune rules the cyclical process of arising (birth), becoming (life), passing away (death) to a new arising (rebirth).

As "The Old English Rune Poem" clearly, if symbolically, indicates, the power of *berkano* is self-contained. It can grow independent of outside forces, but no growth can take place in the natural world without the aid of the self-generated process of the B-rune. *Berkano* takes seed substance, hides or conceals it in its enclosure, breaks the enclosure, and bears the transformed substance forth. It is structurally linked to, though independent of, the NG-rune.

The symbol of the B-rune is the birch rod, the magical instrument through which its powers (of fertility, transformations, eroticism) are evoked in the earth and in humanity.

Cosmologically, : ᛒ : is a "unit of becoming." It is that *moment of being* (a single "micro-cycle" of arising–becoming–passing away) on which all *becoming* is based—the eternal now. The B-rune also describes the principle of phenomenological randomness in the multiverse—chance in the evolutionary process.

Berkano is a conserving, protective force and rules over concealing enclosures (especially those used in transformational rites).

The B-rune also conceals the great mystery of the "alchemy of the word," the power by which words are woven into meanings beyond their concrete definitions. In this, *berkano* is closely allied with *ansuz*. This is understandable because of all goddesses, Freyja is mistress to *all* aspects of the B-rune.

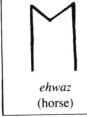

ehwaz
(horse)

This is the rune of the symbiotic relationship between any two systemically distinct yet harmoniously working beings. In ancient times this was most directly perceived in the relationship between a man and his horse, especially among the Indo-Europeans who were the first to train these powerful creatures. *Ehwaz* is the mystery of the dually arrayed and sympathetic forces: man/horse, horse/chariot, and so on.

The E-rune is the *living* vehicle of the runester's journeys in self-transformation: the rune of the *fylgja* itself (not just the force of its attraction : ᛦ :) as a controlled or cooperative entity. That this symbolism is deep rooted is demonstrated by the Old Norse formula *marr er manns fylgja* (the "horse is a man's fetch"). The "horse/man symbiosis" as a metaphor for true human existence (or that of the athling or Erulian) is shown by the bind rune : ᛗ :(*e* + *m(+ k)*, I am). Perhaps most central to the mystery of *ehwaz* is the steed of Óðhinn, Sleipnir (an offspring of Loki). The level of identity between Óðhinn/Sleipnir is indicated by riddle (no. 72) recorded in the *Saga of Heidrek the Wise:*

Who are those two,
that have ten feet,
three eyes
and one tail?

(Answer: Ódhinn riding on Sleipnir)

Ehwaz is the force on which the runester "slips" from one world to another. It is a sign of great loyalty, especially between men and women, and it is a symbol of lawful marriage.

The archetypal force of this rune is still vibrant around us even in popular culture, especially once one realizes that unconsciously the "horse" has become *motorized*. The man/horse/woman "triangle" is virtually cliché.

mannaz
(man)

This is the structure of (divine) consciousness in mankind, imparted there through a genetic link with the unified god of consciousness. This is possessed in varying degrees by humans as described in the "Rígsthula" in the *Poetic Edda*. The link is there because ultimately humans are *descendants* of the gods; that is, the relationship is *genetic* not *contractual*. Hence, it is actually unbreakable.

A god with the name *Mannus* was worshipped in the time of Tacitus (first century C.E.), as there we have the earliest parallel to the Rígr/Heimdallr version of the origin of human society recorded in the "Rígsthula." (See the *Germania*, chapter 2.)

Mannaz is a god made flesh, not as a unique historical event, as Christians would have us believe, but as a great biological, sociological, psychological process of consciousness becoming manifest. This is the mystery underlying the rune poem stanzas having to do with this stave.

The M-rune is the harmonious combination of the "mind" and "memory." In the M-rune Huginn and Muninn speak freely to one another and inform the whole-self of the god Ódhinn (see chapter 12). This is the man made whole, the initiate of the Ódhinic cult (Erulian). In Jungian terms it is the individuated self.

Mannaz is the rune of the moon, and of its tripartite nature: dark ● —becoming ◐ —light ○ . In Germanic lore the moon is masculine (the *man* in the moon) and a transformational essence. It is the synthesis of the intuitive and rational (measuring, analyzing) intelligences in man. Its very name means "the measurer" (of time). As with Ódhinn, his face is always changing, yet it remains always the same.

laguz
(water-lake)

This *laguz* is the primeval cosmic water that wells up from Niflheimr—containing all life-potential—which is transformed into cosmic ice and energized by the fires of Muspellsheimr. It is the ultimate medium for life-containing forces. (See "Cosmogony" in chapter 10.)

Laguz-force "falls" into the realm of manifestation from extradimensional realms (Útgardhr). This downward flow of energy complements the upward flow described in the alternate name of the L-rune, *laukaz* (leek). For this reason, the waterfall is a potent symbol of the dynamic mystery of this rune. It should be noted that the original place of the golden hoard of the Nibelungs was under a waterfall; it is to this myth of mysteries that the second half-line of "The Old Norwegian Rune Rhyme" refers.

The L-rune describes the layers of the laws of life, the layers with which *ørlög* works to form the wyrd of the cosmos and of individual elements within it.

Laguz is the rune of organic life and the passage to and from that state. This "water" is the main element in the mixture (ON *aurr*) that the Norns draw up out of the Well of Urdhr (Wyrd) to preserve the organized life of the World-Tree. At birth the Germanic child is reintegrated into the organic life of its clan through the rite of *vatni ausa* ("sprinkling with water"). Here the noun *aurr* and the verb *ausa* are derived from the same root. Also, the old Germanic funeral rites are often connected with water symbolism (ship burial, ship cremation, burial or cremation within ship-formed stone settings, etc.). The entryways into Hel are conceived of as rivers, with Ódhinn often seen as the ferryman of the souls.

As a rune of life and vital power, *laguz* is closely related to the mystery of *uruz* (by the laws of skaldcraft *uruz* became connected to the concept *aurr*).

The L-rune manifests the unknown, dark depths of the watery, primeval state and that of death. If the runester (seafarer) is fitted out with an unsuitable vehicle (ship), he will fear the ebb and flow of this force. The "brine-steed" must be controlled in order to fare well.

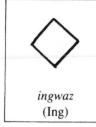

ingwaz
(Ing)

The *ingwaz*-force is that which is released to give the plentiful year (: ◊ :). This is demonstrated in the relationships between their stave shapes. The force that breaks it open is that of *berkano* (: ᛒ :). The NG-rune is the nourishment, the seed energy needed during the period of gestation. The cosmic food is contained and consumed by *berkano* and borne forth through its power to replenish energy lost in the cyclical process.

It should be noted that the NG-stave was originally made smaller than other staves in the row and separate from the sometimes imaginary bottom line of the other staves. It is withdrawn into a hidden and independent realm for the secret exchange of energies that leads to transformation. In the NG-rune is contained the mystery of the transformational process of withdrawal–transformation–return. This process is useful in initiatory rites but is actually a powerful aid in any transformational operation (see figure 9.2).

This process is often experienced intellectually when an idea that is somehow incomplete or imperfect is "put on the back burner" for a while, allowed to gestate in the unconscious (or perhaps better said, in the

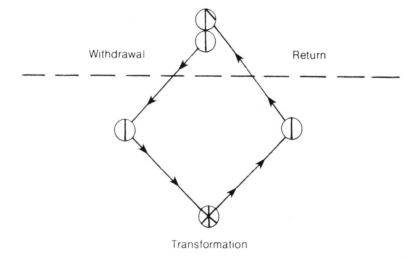

Figure 9.2. Process of transformation

"hyperconscious") to be brought forth as a completed and perfected concept. The aspect of submersion into hidden realms is made quite clear in "The Old English Rune Poem." "Going to the east" is always a code for faring into the realm of the etins, the dark preconscious forces of the cosmos.

dagaz
(day)

The D-rune is the process that takes place at the edges of extremes. As the day and darkness merge in the twilight and the beacons of that tide, the morning and evening stars (for which *Dagaz* [ON *Dagr*] is a name) shine into the realm of Midhgardhr. It is a sign of the light of consciousness borne by Ódhinn-Vili-Vé to mankind by their gift.

In "The Old English Rune Poem" a synthesis between the powers of the drighten (lord = Woden or Ódhinn) and the metod (measurer = Tiw or Týr) is indicated, a synthesis between the right and left brain thinking that is the hallmark of inspiration.

Dagaz is the "Ódhinic Paradox"—the sudden realization (after concerted conscious effort of the will) that perceived opposites are aspects of a third idea that contains them both. This is the mystery of hyperconsciousness central to the Ódhinic cult, the Germanic cult of consciousness. In the light of the D-rune the pathways between extremes are seen clearly. An Odian does not seek the mystery of *dagaz* at the center but rather at the extreme borders. This is the simultaneous, bidirectional will that is almost unique to Germanic magical lore. The search ends when the contents of the extreme borderlands fall into a vortex of single pointed wholeness in the "center" (actually an extradimensional concept).

In : ᛞ : we see the extradimensional models such as the Moebius strip and the toroidal vortex (see figure 9.3), where in becomes out and out

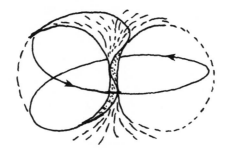

Figure 9.3. Toroidal vortex: Dagaz

becomes in. This is of ultimate importance when considering the nature of the Odian mission in the world.

othala
(odal-land)

Othala is the sacred enclosure. In it is embodied the central concept of Midhgardhr and of the whole idea of "in-sidedness" and "out-sidedness" so prominent in Germanic (and Indo-European) thought. The O-rune describes the ring-wall, the symbol of the enclosed land separated from all that around it and thereby made sacred (ON *vé*). It is a sign of the site set apart for sacred purposes, the fane or hall. For the most part the *othala* force acts as a selective barrier. It prevents forces detrimental to the health of the interior form from entering, but it actually conducts beneficial energies into its interior.

In the often highly mobile society in which the runestaves were developed this concept quickly took on an abstract meaning, that of the spiritual heritage of the clan or tribe of which the odal-enclosure had been a symbol. As such, the O-rune is a sign of the *kynfylgja* (kin-fetch)—the sum of the spiritual heritage of a group. These kin-fetches are inherited from one generation to another and attach themselves to tribal or national leaders (see Runic Psychology, chapter 12). This is a metagenetic concept, and as such cannot as yet be fully explained in physical or purely organic terms. It is a hidden genetic code governed by laws of heredity active in families, clans, tribes, nations—but it goes beyond them as well.

Forces held by the ring of the O-rune must be well ordered and harmonious, following the path of right (: ᚱ :). With this state the common good is provided for, and peace and freedom reign. To this *in*-side, Ódhinn turns his All-fatherly face—but he also faces outward into Útgardhr whence the Odian often draws power and inspiration to serve himself and the good of the folk. But for the non-Odian to be thrust into the outside world—to become outlawed—is tantamount to a death sentence. This is because the non-athling does not have a sense-of-self developed to the stage where he could survive such a psychological shock. Deprived of human context he is obliterated. The O-rune contains all aspects of this mystery.

Othala describes the essence of the mystery of the ebb and flow between states of order and chaos—the great cosmic state of flux. However, it celebrates the state of balance obtained when forces of consciousness have established their enclosures (Ásgardhr and Midhgardhr) interacting with the powers of the exterior darkness (Útgardhr). Ódhinn and his Erulians seek to maintain this balance. All-father is wise enough to know the ultimate outcome—but sly enough to know how to overcome it.

The Runic System

After studying the foregoing rune tables, the reader will be impressed with the degree to which the runes seem to interrelate. Runes weave in and out of one another in a great serpentine interlace of meaning. Indeed, their heritage is as much one of poetry (skaldcraft) as of "science." As in poetry, linkages are made between "words" (here, ideas) through associations on various levels: sounds (rhyme, alliteration, etc.), spatial arrangements (meter), and mythic allusion. Skaldcraft sprang from runecraft, so the similarity in practice is not surprising. It is the intention of the runic system to break down barriers in the consciousness and to reveal the hidden meanings within the worlds. It does this through a sometimes tangled web-work of words and images, each reverberating off the other. Each rune is bound to the other as surely as it has its own unique identity. Certain obscure aspects of the ways the runes relate to each other are explored in the section "Runes" in chapter 10; however, here we will deal with the secrets contained in the most traditional yet mysterious arrangement of the runes in the three *ættir* ("families" or "eights").

There is no "logical" or linguistic reason why the runestaves should be arranged in three groups of eight. This is a feature the Elder Futhark shares with ancient Greek, and there may be some Indo-European mystery of "twenty-four-foldedness" shared from the remote past at work here. Also, even among scholars there is no commonly agreed on reason as to why the runes have actual *meaningful names*. The Greek and Roman alphabets have only nonsensical names, like our letter "names." The idea of having meaningful words as letter names is a feature shared with the celtic ogham and the Hebrew alphabet.

What is known is that the runes remained an organized body of lore that went far beyond the amount of information necessary to keep a simple

Table 9.1. Synthetic Rune Table

f–ehu 1	u–ruz 2	th–urisaz 3	a–nsuz 4	r–aidho 5	k–enaz 6	g–ebo 7	w–unjo 8
h–agalaz 9	n–authiz 10	i–sa 11	j–era 12	ei–hwaz 13	p–erthro 14	elha–z 15	s–owilo 16
t–iwaz 17	b–erkano 18	e–hwaz 19	m–annaz 20	l–aguz 21	ing–waz 22	d–agaz 23	o–thala 24

alphabet system intact for more than a thousand years. When all is said and done, the whole of runelore is summed up in table 9.1.

To unlock this table, we are faced with a double problem. First we must delve into the innate mysteries themselves, but before we can do that we must know a good deal about the basic meanings of these names and configurations. Through comprehension of the ancient lore, knowledge of the timeless mysteries will grow.

The deep-level structure of the multiversal mysteries (runes) is precisely reflected in the outer form of the system of the staves (= runes). This runic system is a complex, sometimes extralinguistic framework of lore that includes

1. individual stave shape
2. phonetic values of staves
3. names of staves
4. explanatory poetic stanza
5. order of staves (= number)
6. tripartite division of staves (*ættir*)

Only the second element of this system is truly necessary for a simple, linguistically functioning alphabet system. All of the rest is there for some other, more mytho-magical reason. In this section we hope to begin to instill in the aspiring runester some of the depth of this system, which underlies all formations and transformations of the runic tradition throughout history.

STAVE SHAPES

As far as the actual shape of individual runestaves is concerned, there seem to have been some variations. However, only rarely did these go beyond what might be called "typological" variants. For example, in the elder period, the S-rune could be represented by forms such as : ⟨ ⟩ ⟨ ⟩ ⟨ ⟩ ⟩ ⟩ —but they all belong to the zig-zag or serpentine type. These principles should be kept in mind when intuitively exploring the inner meaning of the stave shapes. Through history, some never change, whereas others do. There is a hidden significance in this development or lack of it.

PHONETIC VALUES

The sound value of each stave shape is also relatively fixed, with only certain systematic shifts. This second element in the system is actually totally dependent on the third.

STAVE NAMES

These ideologically and culturally loaded names are acrophonic; that is, they indicate the sound value of a stave through the initial sound in the name of the stave, for example, *f-ehu* = [f]. The *names* themselves, however, are to be interpreted on three levels. As the runester will come to understand, this multilevel approach is basic to all illustrative runic work. These three levels are (using *uruz* as our example): (1) the "fundamental" or literal (aurochs—a large and powerful, wild four-legged beast), (2) the esoteric or metaphorical, often socio-mythological (aurochs—the primeval bovine of formation); (3) the runo-Erulian, often runo-psychological (aurochs—the circulation of vital forces in consciousness and the capacity to understand).[2]

The name contains the idea and the sound. It is highly probable that there existed in ancient times a complex *system* of names, and that each rune had a group of words (possibly three) that could be used as its names. The Rune-Gild is slowly recovering these, but here we deal with the primary names and their meanings, shown in Table 9.2.

Anyone with an active interest in the runes will want to begin to make certain associations among and between runes on all levels. What shapes are related to what other shapes and how? What names are related to what other names and on what levels? On this last point it will be noticed, for example, that these primary rune names are drawn from certain areas of life: (1) the superhuman realms: *ansuz, thurisaz, tiwaz, ingwaz,* and perhaps *berkano*; (2) organic nature: *fehu, uruz, eihwaz, elhaz,* and *mannaz*; (3) inorganic nature: *hagalaz, isa, jera, sowilo, laguz,* and *dagaz*; (4) technology: *raidho, kenaz, perthro,* and possibly *nauthiz*; and (5) cultural realms: *gebo, wunjo,* and *othala*. These categories can be further analyzed and recombined to give deeper meanings.

---

[2] Thorsson, *Futhark: A Handbook of Rune Magic*, chap. 2.

Table 9.2. Stave Names and Meanings*

fehu (f)	domesticated cattle, livestock, unit of monetary value, FEE
uruz (u)	AUROCHS, wild horned beast
thurisaz (th)	THURS (primal giant), thing of great strength
ansuz (a)	an ancestral sovereign god (the Ase, Ódhinn)
raidho (r)	wagon, RIDE
kenaz (k)	torch (secondary name, *kaunaz* [sore])
gebo (g)	GIFT, hospitality
wunjo (w)	joy, ecstasy
hagalaz (h)	HAIL(stone)
nauthiz (n)	NEED, necessity; need-fire
isa (i)	ICE
jera (j)	(the good) year; harvest
eihwaz (ei/i)	YEW
perthro (p)	lot cup
elhaz (-z)	ELK (secondary name, *algiz* [protection])
sowilo (s)	sun
tiwaz (t)	(the god) Týr (OE Tiw)
berkano (b)	the BIRCH (goddess)
ehwaz (e)	horse (see Latin *equus*)
mannaz (m)	MAN
laguz (l)	water (LAKE)
ingwaz (ng)	(the god) Ing
dagaz (d)	DAY
othala (o)	ancestral (ODAL) property

*Words in capitals indicate modern English *cognates*, i.e., words that are directly derived from the ancient terms.

Runic Arrangements

The ordering of the twenty-four runes gives each stave a numerical position in the series 1 to 24, and the division of these twenty-four into three segments results in groupings of eight. These numerical formulas are innate in the runic system. When the system was reformed in the Viking Age, it was done by a systematic reduction of these numerical formulas.[3]

All runes came into being simultaneously, and each is linked to the other on different levels. The most obvious linkages are seen in the ordering and *ætt* divisions ("airts"). Indeed, on *one* level, *fehu* is related to *uruz*, which is linked to *thurisaz*, and so forth in a straight line 1 to 24. This line is divided into three in such a way that each group of eight (*ætt*) also shares certain characteristics, and in addition this results in eight groups of three runes vertically arranged (e.g., : ᚠ :/: ᚺ :/: ↑ :) that are also bonded in a special way. It should also be noted that even on the horizontal 1 to 24 series, groups of three (1–3, 4–6, etc.) are significant. For the active runester these can serve as excellent subjects of meditation and contemplation.

The underlying meanings of the three airts are clear. The first airt delineates the mysteries the runester must learn and master before setting out on the difficult path of the Odian. This airt shows the establishment of the basic talents and characteristics of the runester: energy, understanding, action, inspiration, ritual, controlled will, generosity, and fellowship. It corresponds to the dreng. The second airt is twofold and full of trial and tribulation. H to J outline the process of overcoming objective confrontations and gaining the good harvest from them, and EI to S describe the subjective conflicts and the pathway to success. This corresponds to the work of the thegn. The third airt (of Týr) describes the realm in which the Erulian, or runemaster, works. Established at the summit of the world column (: ↑ :) and able to generate his own power internally along the pathways of the tree (: ᛒ :), the runemaster, in tandem with his self-created and integrated divine "ego" (: ᛗ :), is able to pass through all layers of existence (: ᛚ :) to become the, independent, self-contained, and ever evolving Erulian god-man (: ◇ :) enlightened by the "light" of day (: ᛞ :), ever interacting with the world "outside" while remaining above and beyond the fray (: ᛟ :). This is the work of the drighten.

---

[3] For the further cosmological significance of these orderings see chap. 10 of this volume; see also Edred Thorsson, *Futhark: A Handbook of Rune Magic* (York Beach, ME: Samuel Weiser, 1984): chap. 3.

As the next chapter will make clearer, the runes actually belong to a fourth-dimensional reality, and therefore all attempts to represent them or their relationships must fall short. Ultimately, the runes can be seen clearly only in the "light" of *dagaz*. Through weaving the great web-work of mysteries, and thereby "worming" along the ways toward conscious realization of hidden realities, the runester will emerge and wing his way toward the Gard of the Gods.

Esoteric Cosmology
(Birth of the Worlds)

Under the heading of *cosmogony* we will also discuss theogony (birth of the gods) and anthropogony (birth of man), each in its turn. In the *Gylfaginning* (chapters 5–9) we read in great detail how the world was wrought. The description given there tells of the watery realm of Niflheimr (Mist-World) in the north, out of which flowed the ice streams loaded with yeasty venom, and of Muspellsheimr (Fire-World) in the south, out of which flew fire and sparks. These two extremes of energy flowed toward each other through *Ginnunga-gap* (Magically Charged Space). The extremes on either side brought about a harmonious condition in the center of Ginnungagap; and as the sparks and hot air of Muspellsheimr hit the ice, it quickened the yeast within it, and a form was shaped from the union of these energies—Ymir (the Roarer).

From Ymir are descended the rime-thurses. As a bisexual being, Ymir engendered a male and female thurs under his left hand, and one of his feet engendered a son with the other foot.

As a part of the same process in which Ymir came about, Audhumla, the cosmic bovine, was shaped as a coagulation of the dripping rime. She gave nourishment to Ymir with the milk that flowed from her udders. She, in turn, was fed directly from the frozen drizzle, by licking a salty ice block

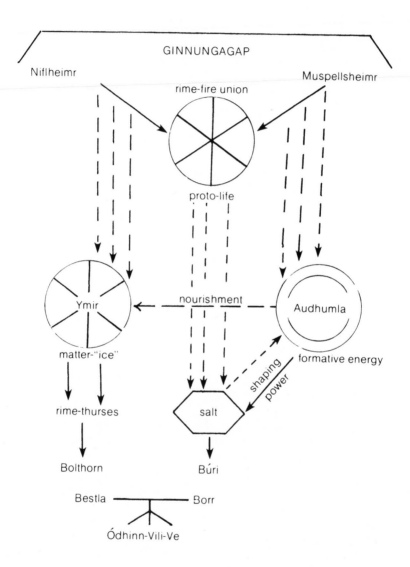

Figure 10.1. Cosmogonic process

formed by it. From this block, she licked the form of a being named Búri. Búri, an androgynous entity, engendered a son called Borr, who subsequently married an etin-wife named Bestla, the daughter of an etin named Bölthorn (Evil-thorn). From the union of the proto-god Borr and the etin-wife Bestla, the divine triad Ódhinn-Vili-Vé was born.

This godly triad then set about to kill (sacrifice) Ymir. This they did and took his form to the middle of Ginnungagap, and from this substance they fitted out the framework of the multiverse. They gave shape to the world and set the mechanisms of the world in motion within the context of the four quarters. The heavens were shaped from Ymir's skull, at the four corners of which the gods set four dwarves—Nordhri, Austri, Sudhri, and Vestri. At the very center they built a stonghold from the brows of Ymir, which was called Midhgardhr (the Middle-Yard).

Now the divine triad set about shaping mankind. This was done as Ódhinn-Vili-Vé were in Midhgardhr near the sea, where they found two trees. To these already living beings Ódhinn gave *önd* (spirit, the breath of life), Vili gave *ódhr* inspired mental activity), and Vé gave form, speech, and the senses. This process is also described with the divine triad Ódhinn-Hœnir-Lódhurr in the "Völuspá" (sts. 17–18) in the *Poetic Edda*. The male being was called Askr (ash) and the female Embla (elm).

This text should be read by all students and meditated upon deeply. It contains many runic mysteries.

The whole cosmogonic/theogonic proto-process is schematized in figure 10.1, which conceptualizes the entire primordial evolutionary complex as seen by the ancient Germanic peoples. This can be only an approximation, however, because the actual process is multidimensional.

Ginnungagap is a space charged with a field of proto-energy. Niflheimr and Muspellsheimr constitute that energy in a highly polarized and intensified state, which then interacts with itself in the center, where a new formation modeled on innate multiversal patterning is manifested. This is symbolized by : ✳ :, which is the pattern of the World-Tree as an ultimate crystallization of this seed pattern. It is also the snowflake pattern, which demonstrates the nature of these unmanifested images to become visible once they are fed with the proper energies and substances. The fiery realm is a manifestation of the light energy of maximal vibration, whereas the icy realm is a solidification of the dark energy containing the elemental kernel of the mysteries of life and death—yeast, salt, and venom.

Once this proto-seed form is shaped, it splits into another polarization of proto-matter (Ymir) and proto-energy (Audhumla), but some of the energy from the proto-seed falls into Ginnungagap and is recrystallized as the ice block from which the proto-energy exercises its shaping power to form the androgynous proto-god/etin, Búri. Búri contains the pure pattern from the direct union of fire and ice but is shaped by the forces of proto-energy itself (and gives of itself in a form of self-sacrifice to the cosmic bovine). Ymir, the mass of raw cosmic material and the innate cosmic form or pattern contained in the "seed of ice"—the hailstone (*hagall* : ᚼ :)—is ultimately sacrificed by a triad of divine beings (i.e., the forms of primal consciousness). These three beings—truly a whole—are the first conscious, and therefore divine, beings because they can comprehend dualities and shape their environment due to the innate synthetic consciousness that results from their descent from a triple source: (1) the primal seed union, (2) Ymir, and (3) Audhumla. The triad of consciousness dissolves Ymir, and out of its matter reshapes the static cosmos into a dynamic, living, and conscious organization, according to the *right* (i.e., innate) patterns already contained in the matter itself (Ymir) and in the primal seed.

Humanity is a further shaping by the conscious divinities. But again, humanity is a part of the whole of the cosmos, not something *created (ex nihilo)* by the "gods." Askr and Embla were already living beings (organic: here symbolized as plants), and the complex artificially expanded consciousness was imparted to them (co-equally and simultaneously) as a part of the non-natural evolution of consciousness in Midhgardhr.

Runes

The runes themselves define the patterns of existence and of consciousness; therefore, they are at work throughout the cosmogonic process. Before the sacrifice of Ymir, those patterns are unmanifested, and only in a rudimentally differentiated state. Only the biune duality between the murk runes (ON *myrkrúnar*) and the shining runes (ON *heidhrúnar*) was manifest. The runes bloom forth into an independent and isolated state upon the birth of Ódhinn-Vili-Vé (when the murk and shining runes are entirely resynthesized into a whole coherent system). The runes, as we can begin to know them, are manifested in divine consciousness and in world being. When the triad of consciousness sacrificed Ymir (the crystallized seed of runic pattern), they *shaped* this primal substance according to the inherent runic structure. They arranged it in the shape of the Nine Worlds of Yggdrasill (see figure 10.7 on page 154).

It must be borne in mind that these "events" take place in dimension(s) beyond our three, and as such, processes that we must discuss in a sequence may be "synchronistic." So it is with "events" of the birth of Ódhinn-Vili-

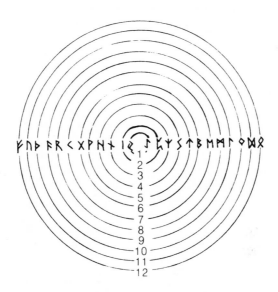

Figure 10.2. Diagram of the futhark pattern of manifestation

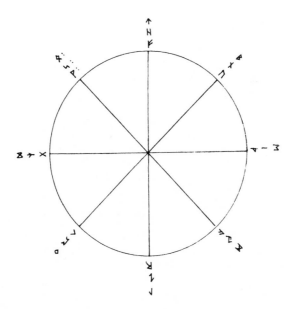

Figure 10.3. Eightfold division of the futhark

Vé, the sacrifice of Ymir, the manifestation of the runes and the world (Yggdrasill), and the rune-winning initiation of Ódhinn (see Runelore of the Gods, chapter 13). On different levels these events all describe one face: consciousness enters the organic order from outside that order.

As far as the (re)birth of the runic system is concerned, this manifests itself through the processes of (1) the blooming forth of the runes from a central point in a bidirectional or twofold spherical pattern (see figure 10.2 on page 147) and (2) the wrapping of the resulting sequence around an eightfold plane (see figure 10.3). This gives the runes an organization that is comprehensible and communicable. It provides order and orientation.

The first unfolding from a central point begins with the two kernel, or "core," rune forms of cyclical (: ◊ :) and vertical (: ↑ :) force—the cycles of becoming and the axis of being. Thus, according to the patterns of the mystery of twenty-four, the runes manifest within a twelvefold sphere; each rune aligns with another according to a "law" of sympathy/antipathy as the spheres expand. The numerical sequence 1 to 24 is crystallized upon the application of the ordering force of consciousness that organizes the runes from left to right (in the *natural* order, i.e., along the pathway of the sun). It

Table 10.1. Runic Dyads

Sphere Number	Rune Forms	Cosmogonic Characteristics
1	◊ : ↑	orbit/axis
2	I : ᚴ	contraction/evolution
3	↓ : ↓	resistance/attraction
4	ᚻ : ᛋ	seed form/light crystal
5	ᛈ : ↑	harmony/order
6	ᚷ : ᛒ	exchange/retention
7	ᚲ : ᛗ	ability/trust
8	ᚱ : ᛗ	cosmic order/human order
9	ᚠ : ᚱ	transformation/growth
10	ᚦ : ◊	breaker/container
11	ᚢ : ᛞ	formation/paradox
12	ᚴ : ᛉ	mobile power/immobile power

must be remembered, however, that runes could be carved in *any* direction—left to right, right to left, or back and forth. These facts show the way to a deeper understanding of the hidden meanings behind this practice. The spherical ordering of the futhark is graphically represented in figure 10.2. The significance of the dyadic parings of the runes that result from this pattern of "blooming forth" shown in figure 10.2 is indicated in table 10.1.

From the previous chapter it is known that the harmonious arrangement of the runes in *ættir* is a significant mystery in and of itself. As the runes are ordered in their sequence 1 to 24, they emerge into the horizontal plane of existence from the "north" (that is, out of the doorway to other worlds) and, like a serpent, wrap themselves three times about the circular plane around Midhgardhr. In the Germanic tradition, planes are divided into eight segments in order to gain a position or orientation on that plane. These eight segments or divisions are called *ættir* (which can mean *both* "families" and "eights," i.e., the "eight directions"). (An archaic Scots dialect word *airt* survives in this meaning.) It is probably from this cosmological pattern (see figure 10.3) that the primary significance of the airt divisions of the futhark was derived.

Yet a third basic "arrangement" of the runes, one which emphasizes the multidimensional reality of the mysteries in the branches of Yggdrasill, will be discussed later.

Runic Elements

The subject of elements in the runic context has been one of the most hotly pursued areas of speculation and inner work among those dedicated to the Ódhinic path. This in large measure is due to the prominent role played by the four elements of air, fire, water, and earth in the Hermetic/Neo-Platonic school of occult philosophy to which the runic is often compared, or out of which it loosened itself in more recent times. These Neo-Platonic elements may very well derive from some formalization of Indo-European patterns, and these may indeed have been shared by the Germanic peoples. The elements are essentially basic classes of substances occurring in nature that evoke certain subjective psychic responses when meditated on. They are classificatory tools for the psychophysical complex. As such, it seems most beneficial to explore the runic ideology to extract from it directly, through runic investigation (a combination of lore learning and "wizardry"), the nature of the mysteries of *runic elements*. Here a note must be interjected: although what follows is based on traditional sources, it is not intended as a dogmatic rule. Other interpretations may be possible. It is hoped that this work will open some doors and at least broaden somewhat those doors that have long stood wide.

As far as the lore is concerned, the secrets of the *Eddas* have for too long been ignored. In them is housed a great wealth of hidden knowledge if one will only open one's eyes to it. The cosmogonic myth explored at the beginning of this chapter holds the keys to the secrets of the ancient and complex science of runic elements.

The polarized primary elements are two in number: (1) fire and (2) ice, and the secondary ones are (3) water and (4) air. Further elemental building blocks of life are also described in the *Gylfaginning* in the *Prose Edda*: (5) iron (slag and the "sparks" from Muspellsheimr as its heat reaches the center), (6) salt, (7) yeast, (8) venom. These are all synthesized in the final element—(9) earth. All of these elements work on the "plane of manifestation"—the horizontal plane—not on the vertical axis of consciousness. These elements are meaningfully diagrammed in figure 10.4. A short description of the nature of each element, read in conjunction with the cosmogonic myth, and with comprehension of the runic system will help in the understanding of this complex:

Fire: Total expansion, all-vibration, heat, light, dryness, proto-energy—dynamic.
Ice: Total contraction, nonvibration, coldness, darkness, proto-matter—dynamic.
Water: Stillness, evolutionary being, wetness, matrix for form—static.
Air: All pervasiveness, formless space, warm, matrix for consciousness—static.
Iron: Primary synthesis, hot/cold, hard, dynamically penetrating, inert matter.
Salt: "Stuff of life" and substance of organic life, maintainer of form.
Yeast: Dynamic "livingness," organic movement, growth, health.
Venom: Latent dissolution, corrosiveness, organic dynamism (negative evolutionary factor—destruction necessary to reshaping).
Earth: All-potential, manifestation, final elemental synthesis.

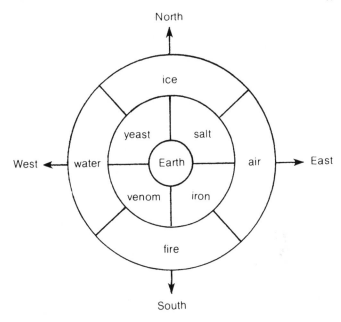

Figure 10.4. Runic elements on the horizontal plane

These must not be interpreted as "emanations" of one another. All elements are real and latent in the whole, in the universe (omniverse), before they are manifested in the multiverse.

The primary dyad fire:ice interacts across the expanse of the *gap* (filled with *ginnung*, proto-consciousness, which will "solidify" in the vertical axis), and those dynamic all-extremes call forth the balancing, mediating factors of the secondary dyad water:air. The interaction of these elements gives rise to the whole of the organic processes. At the most direct, least mediated contact point between fire and ice, primal iron is forged in the cosmic crucible, and its primary and most purely "elemental" synthesis of fire:ice interacts like a lightning bolt with the latent organic mixture of yeast/salt/venom within the matrix of fire:ice/water:air. This spark of life first quickens the yeast, causing the organic birth process to be set in motion. This is eternally maintained by the salt of life, which holds the process together. However, the latent venom ensures the continued dynamism and evolutionary nature of the process because it is continually dissolving life so that it may be reshaped in ever more complex forms by consciousness. Here

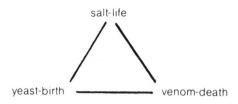

Figure 10.5. Elemental cycle of becoming

we see the origins of the material aspects of the "high-holy-three" (trifidic-truine dyad)—birth-life-death to rebirth (as in figure 10.5).

All of these factors go into the formation and quickening of the center of the horizontal plane, the middle of the *gap* where all conditions are ideal for ultimate development and reproduction of the whole—the *earth*. This is also the center point of the numinous vertical axis of the world, which completes its potential for the realization of the whole.

These seem only to constitute a first level of runic elemental wisdom. Actually, the elemental factors could probably be multiplied and refined more and more (as they have been by the physical sciences) to construct a veritable "periodic table" of runic elements. The roots of such a system are shown in figure 10.6.

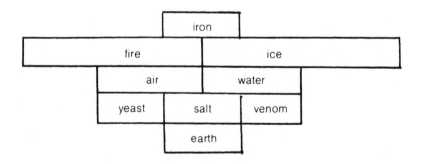

Figure 10.6. Table of runic elements

The employment of "elemental thinking" in the development of a true philosophy—which takes into account not only consciousness but also the natural world and the building of symbolic and psychological bridges between the two—is of invaluable aid. This is because the conscious analysis, categorization, and experience of readily apparent physical phenomena leads to an internalization process with regard to the environment, so that nature can indeed become a loremaster in a living way and the path toward the whole will become clearer.

Yggdrasill

Once the gods have shaped the cosmos from the primal substance according to its pattern and set the whole in motion, so that it becomes a living, organic, evolving thing, the whole is viewed as a cosmic tree— Yggdrasill. The descriptions of the world structure given in the *Eddas* does not always provide a totally consistent picture, but we do not expect one in a multiversal system. The enigma and mystery housed in metaphors show us that these are observations of the travelers in the supraconscious, the true shamans, and not the dogmatic constructs of rationalistic philosophers. However, at present we have need and use for these schematizations to help us unwrap some of the enigma enshrouding the cosmos. Therefore, we must now explore the esoteric analytically before delving into the uncharted waters of Niflheimr. The approximations of such schemata must always be borne in mind.

From the *Prose Edda* and our knowledge of the Nine Worlds of Yggdrasill, we can build a primary structure of the cosmos. But in and around these worlds (ON *heimar*; sg., *heimr*) there are many dwellings, and the *Eddas* speak of them in many passages.

We know that Midhgardhr (the manifested "material" world) is in the *middle* of Ginnungagap; that is, it is not, as some occult philosophies would have us believe, at the bottom of the universe. To the north is Niflheimr, to the south, Muspellsheimr; to the east lies Jötunheimr (Etin-World), and to the west is Vanaheimr (Vanir-World). Along a central (but omnipresent)

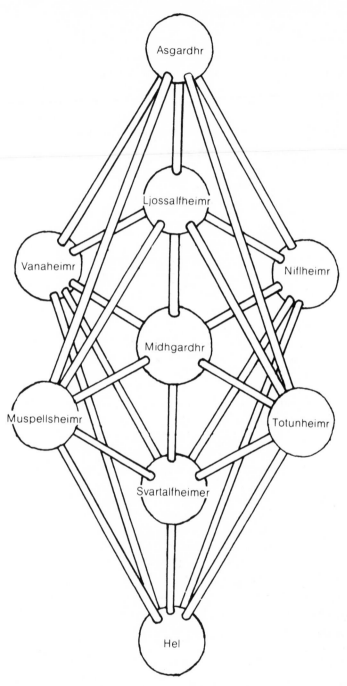

Figure 10.7. Yggdrasill

axis—the Irminsūl—running through the center of Midhgardhr, the realms "above" and "below" Midhgardhr are arranged. It must be remembered that these directions are symbolic of eternal and omnipresent mysteries. Below Midhgardhr is Svartálfheimr (Black-Elf[= dwarf]-World), and below that is Hel (= enclosure of death, the hidden place, the stead of stillness). Above Midhgardhr is Ljóssálfheimr (Light-Elf-World, or simply Elf-World), and above that is Ásgardhr itself (the enclosure of the Æsir). These Nine Worlds are thus arranged along the plan of Yggdrasill and the three-dimensional snowflake pattern. Figure 10.7 gives a detailed description of the mysteries the mysteries of Yggdrasill. This pattern consists of a horizontal plane, described by Muspellsheimr–Niflheimr–Vanaheimr–Jötunheimr–Midhgardhr, and a vertical axis described by Midhgardhr–Ljóssálfheimr–Svartálfheimr–Ásgardhr–Hel. Actually, the center plane should be tilted in the imagination so that Niflheimr is on the nether edge and Muspellsheimr is on the higher one. We know that this is an old conception because linguistic evidence shows that the root word from which "north" is derived (*ner-) originally meant "under." Above Midhgardhr is the realm of light—"the heavens"; below is the world of darkness—"the nether world." And the Irminsūl, the cosmic pillar of Yggdrasill connects them all. M. Eliade's book, *Myth of the Eternal Return*, speaks most eloquently of this mystery. The vertical column or axis defines the psychocosmic bisection between the conscious and unconscious, between light and dark, just as the horizontal plane defines the bisection between the expansive, electric energies of fire and the constrictive, magnetic energies of ice. The horizontal is energy and the plane in which "physical" energy is found; the vertical is the psychic pattern of consciousness and being. All meet in potential harmony in Midhgardhr. This potential can be activated by the runester.

It will be noted that between these Nine Worlds there are *twenty-four* pathways. This has two meanings. It indicates that the mystery of twenty-four helps shape and hold the entire cosmos together (as it formulates the structure of the runic system itself), and on a certain level it indicates that runestaves could be ascribed to the various roads as keys to unlock conscious access to them. Experience has shown that there may be no objective one-to-one correspondence between a runestave and a roadway, although speculative exercises in this direction have always proved meaningful. The universal truth seems to be that the structure of Yggdrasill and that of the runic system are shaped by the same twenty-four-fold force and that each pathway contains an entire potential futhark within it. In the ebb and flow of energies within the system one rune may dominate a certain roadway, but that does not mean other runes are not to be found there. As is usual with the

Table 10.2. Keys to the Worlds of Yggdrasill

Ásgardhr	Realm of consciousness that is in and of itself complex, with many enclosures and halls within it, among them Valhöll (Walhalla), Hall of the Fallen. The abode of the fetch, and the house of the spirit (ON *önd*).
Ljóssalfheimr	Broad expanses of light (which also contain other sub-planes). The abode of mind and memory—the intellect.
Midhgardhr	Middle-Earth. In the Cosmos this is material manifestation—*earth*. In the makeup of man this is the body, but also the all-potential of the self. In Midhgardhr all the worlds meet.
Svartálfheimr	Abode of the *hamr* (shape or hide). A "subterranean" world of darkness where shapes are forged. Realm of the emotions.
Hel	Realm of the instincts. Abode of stillness and inertia—unconsciousness. The final resting place of the soul of the non-Erulian.
Niflheimr	Realm of mist becoming ice, abode of contraction and magnetism. The force of antimatter, a point constantly pulling in on itself, like a "black hole."
Muspellsheimr	Realm of fiery sparks, abode of expansion and electricity. The force of pure energy constantly expanding away from itself.
Vanaheimr	Realm of organic patterning and coalescence—water. Abode of forces in fruitful and static balance.
Jötunheimr	A realm in constant motion, seeking to oppose and give resistance to whatever it meets. Force of dissolution and deception. Reactive power of destruction (necessary to evolutionary change).

runes, much is dependent on the state of being of the runester—the observer of the mysteries.

As far as analyzing the essences of the worlds is concerned, table 10.2 provides the fundamental esoteric lore necessary to the runic comprehension of the realms of Yggdrasill.

These worlds and enclosures interact with one another in a cosmic ecology of energy and essence. The eight realms outside Midhgardhr each oppose and balance a counter realm: Ásgardhr balances Hel, Ljóssalfheimr balances Svartálfheimr, Muspellsheimr (fire) counters Niflheimr (ice, and Vanaheimr counters Jötunheimr. The "material world," Midhgardhr, stands in the midst of all—the realm of all-potential. From it the runester can reach out in all directions and ascend to the realms above or ride down to the worlds below. However, it should be noted that there is a special relationship between Ásgardhr, Midhgardhr, and Hel, which are properly called "the three realms"—heavenly, earthly, and chthonic. There is a similar bond among those six realms properly called *heimar*, which "surround" Midhgardhr. Access to realms beyond these six into the outermost two is difficult, to say the least.

Collectively, the pathways between the worlds are known as Bifröst, the Rainbow Bridge. The structure is a model of the world, but it also the pattern of the "world within"—the microcosm of man if you will. This is made abundantly clear in the skaldic language of the north in which humans are often paraphrased in terms of *trees*; for example, a warrior will be called "the oak of battle." These "kennings" are derived from the mythic fact that humans were "shaped" from trees (i.e., already living, organic substance) by the triad of divine consciousness. (Compare this to other mythologies in which humans are fashioned from inert matter.) In the Yggdrasill pattern we have the ancient Germanic (and perhaps even Indo-European) model of the subjective universe and a model for its linkages to the objective universe. Here continues to be hidden a rune of great power.

Runic Numerology

If one has access to the voluminous scholarly works on rune magic, one is at once struck by the abundance of numerological interpretations. Underlying these studies seems to be the assumption that mere numerical patterns (real or imagined) are enough to indicate the "magical" nature of an inscription. The weakness of these works lies in the fact that the authors never tell us *how* these patterns are magically effective, nor do they tell us much of the indigenous Germanic number lore that would be necessary to understand these inscriptions in this way. From a purely historical point of view, it even seems doubtful that runes were ever used as numerals at all. No clear example of such usage exists, and when numbers are expressed in the inscriptions, they are always *spelled out in words*. (This is not to say that there was no sacred or magical tradition of number lore that was a thing altogether separate from the use of "profane" numbers.) The runo-numerological scholars believe that the runemasters of old used both rune counts (counting the total number of staves in an inscription, line, or phrase; e.g., : ᚠ ᚱ ᚼ := 3) or rune totals (counting the total of the numerical values assigned to the staves by virtue of their positions in the row; e.g., : ᚠ ᚱ ᚼ := 4 + 21 + 2 = 27).

The question arises: are these practices legitimate in view of the general lack of historical evidence for them? The answer is yes on two grounds: (1)

the historical evidence generally has been handled badly, and the scientific case (especially for rune counts) needs to be kept open; and (2) in the spirit of living innovation consistently expressed by the elder runemasters, we new runesters should feel free to incorporate and develop tally lore in our system regardless of its historical position. It is not our aim merely to copy older practices but rather to extend them in ways harmonious with the tradition.

Our treatment of runic numerology, or tally lore, is informed by deep knowledge of the uniquely Germanic number lore (usually ignored by earlier scholars in favor of foreign systems) and by the spirit of intuitive innovation.

Tally Lore

Numerical patterning makes an inscription more effective in the realms corresponding to those indicated by the key number. This is simply a part of the laws of systemic empathy necessary to magical working in general. The willed act of consciously shaping operative communications on ever more subtle levels has a powerful intrinsic effect for magical work. In other words, for a magical working to be effective it must be in a form—a code if you will—that the object of the working will be able to "understand" and respond to. Numerical patterning is a subtle level of this encoding process. This is one of the more obscure parts of the answer to the Odian question "Knowest how to carve?"

On the other hand, there is an important passive side to this active aspect. One must also be able to answer the question "Knowest how to read?" That is, the runester must be able to understand the runes when they are presented to him—to the mind's eye, as well as to the body's eye. Therefore, skill at tally lore is also a tool for subtle, illuminative magical work (runecasting).

One thing that has always kept rune tally lore from becoming fully effective has been the general effort to try to make it fit into Mediterranean numerology as practiced by the Greeks, Hebrews, and others. Although the Germanic number system is similar to that used by the Greeks (both being ultimately derived from Indo-European), there is an important shift of emphasis from two to three and its multiples that results in a quasi-duodecimal system for the Germanic peoples. This is why we have "eleven" and "twelve" and not, as we would expect, something like "onteen" and "twenteen." There is an underlying system with an emphasis on twelve and its multiples in the ancient Germanic number system, one that also underlies the tally lore of the runes. When an ancient Saxon in England heard *hundred*, he thought of, in our terms, 120 "things"—*teontig* (ten-ty = 100), *end-leofantig*, (eleven-ty = 110), and so on. This latter term even survives in some southern American dialects as "elebenty."

That number values were in some measure a part of the ancient runic tradition is obvious from the nature of the systems of runic codes (see chapter 7). The runic system, as discussed in chapter 9, and the whole of runic cosmology have a strong numerical basis. Within the runic system certain key numbers stand out. Three and its multiples are obvious—the three airts (*ættir*) of the runestave, for example. Three is an essential cosmic binding number on the vertical numinous axis, a formula that connects what is "above" and "below" with the here and now. Three and all of its multiples contain this root value.

Four and eight have a similar effect on the horizontal plane of nature. The symbolism of these number groups is already clear when one looks at the airt arrangement of the runestaves.

In a spherical and multidimensional sense, the numbers twelve and thirteen are of central importance (see chapter 10). These are at the core of the runic system, and each contains a unique and distinct mystery. In other words, thirteen is not merely twelve plus one. The essence of thirteen is something independent of twelve (this is the central "breaking point" in both the runic system and in the Germanic number system).

The ultimate number of wholeness is twenty-four. It contains a sense of entirety, although it is also subject to significant multiplications. In this regard, the formula $24 \times 3 = 72$ seems to be of particular importance. This value of wholeness for twenty-four was even retained once the system had been reformed. One of the greatest testaments to this fact is the mysterious "twenty-four things" on which runes are to be carved in Sigrdrífa's instructions to Sigurdhr (see the "Sigrdífumál" in the *Poetic Edda*).

Essentially, there are four systemic key numbers: thirteen, sixteen, eighteen, and twenty-four. Each expresses an aspect of totality. In addition, all prime numbers—those that are independent, free, and isolated unto themselves—express an aspect of the magical will of the runester.

Nordic Number Lore

To some extent the runic tables of interpretation[1] reveal a good deal of lore concerning the meanings of number and numerical relationships among the runes. However, as a detailed reading of the oldest texts of Germanic lore shows, there are certain specific powers of characteristics of numbers that the aspiring runester should know. These characteristics are quite often different from those of Mediterranean numerology.

One (1) is the number of beginnings of root causes and solitary force. It is rare in operative runecraft and in mythological references.

Two (2) is the number of cooperation of the redoubled working of tandem forces. In operative work it is sometimes used to strengthen, especially physically. In mythological lore it shows the power of teamwork between complementary pairs: Huginn/Muninn, Geri/Freki (Ódhinn's wolves), Árvakr/Alsvidhr (team of horses that pulls the Sun's wain), or the divine tandem Ódhinn/Loki.

Three (3) is a "holy number" that is vastly represented in lore. It indicates a complete functioning process *process* and is the root force of dynamism. In runecraft, three is used to complete and to quicken things—to move things to action. In the mythic lore three's abound; for example, Urdhr-Verdhandi-Skuld, Ódhinn-Vili-Vé, the three "roots" of Yggdrasill, and the three containers of the poetic mead, Ódhrœrir-Són-Bodhn.

Four (4) is a number of stasis, of solidity and waiting. It *contains* power, and this is one of its chief operative uses. In myth we learn of the four harts that chew the leaves of Yggdrasill and of four dwarves Nordhri–Austri–Sudhri–Vestri at the four cardinal directions.

Five (5) is the number of ordered time and space. The ancient Germanic week was five nights long—called in Old Norse a *fimmt*—which was also the interval of time one had to respond to a legal summons. It is rarely found in mythological lore, but for operative purposes it is a powerful invocatory formula.

[1] See chap. 9 of this volume; see also Edred Thorsson, *Futhark: A Handbook of Rune Magic* (York Beach, ME: Samuel Weiser, 1984): chap. 2.

Six (6) is the number of vibrant life and strength. This can be used to create or destroy. It is rarely found in mythic contexts.

Seven (7) is the number of death and passive contact with the "other worlds." A seven-night interval (ON *sjaund*) is traditional between death and the performance of funeral rites. Not often seen in mythology. Some mythic occurrences seem to have been influenced by astrological lore.

Eight (8) is the number of complete manifestation of wholeness and perfect symmetry. Its chief significance can be found in the eightfold division of the heavens (see chapter 6). It is the number of spatial ordering. Eight is abundant in mytho-magical lore, mainly as a way to list things, for example, the eight woes and their remedies. ("Hávamál," 137), the eight runic operations ("Hávamál," 144), and the eight "best things" ("Grímnismál," 45). All of these texts are to be found in the *Poetic Edda*.

Nine (9) is the "holiest of numbers" and the root of psycho-cosmic powers. It lends its force to any purpose. It is the number of life eternal and death unending. Nine transforms what it touches, yet it remains eternal within itself. Its use abounds in myth and magic. Just to name a few of many examples of the use of nine: nine are the worlds of Yggdrasill, nine are the nights Ódhinn hangs upon it and is thereafter taught nine mighty songs, nine is the number in which the *valkyrjur* often appear to the Erulian.

The two main ways in which runes may be manipulated as numbers are outlined in an operative context in *Futhark* (especially on pp. 102–104). These two methods involve computing the rune count (by adding the number of runestaves) and the rune total (by adding the numerical values of each of the runestaves). For example, one side of a famous and complex runic formula from around 500 C.E. (the Lindholm amulet) may be seen in figure 11.1.

Figure 11.1. Side B of the Lindholm amulet

The rune count usually indicates the realm in which the formula is to work, and the rune total shows the subtle aim or final willed outcome of the formula. These two numbers are further analyzed by adding their digits to come up with a "tally" key number (reduced to a number between one and twenty-four) and by finding multiple values to arrive at "multiple" key numbers. These numbers refine the values already demonstrated by the rune count and total, and show the "magical instruments" by which they work. For example, an analytical table for side B of the Lindholm amulet appears in table 11.1.

By using these subtle ways to "read the runes aright," we see that in the most esoteric terms the inscription in figure 11.1 expresses the pure ordered (5) will of an Erulian vitki (47) working with craft (6) within the whole objective universe (24) toward manifestation (10).

To conclude this chapter on number we must speak to the most mysterious example of numerical symbolism in Germanic literature: stanza 24 of the "Grímnismál" in the *Poetic Edda*, which reads:

> Five hundred doors
> and forty withall,
> I know to be in Valhöll:
> eight hundred lone-warriors [ON *einherjar*]
> go through a lone door
> when they fare forth to fight the wolf [= Fenrir].

Many scholars and mystics alike have been struck by this stanza. One one level the numerical analysis would seem to be 540 × 800 = 432,000— which just happens to be the number of years in the Kali Yuga in the scheme of Hindu cosmology. This has led historians to conclude that there may have

Table 11.1. Numerical Analysis of Lindholm Amulet (B)

Rune count	24	realm of working
tally key	6	
multiple key	4 × 6	way it works in realm
Rune total	235	aim of working
tally key	10	
multiple key	5 × 47	way it reaches its aim

been a good deal of borrowing of ideas from Indo-Iranian culture in the North, or that we are faced with an example of ancient Indo-European lore common to both cultures from prehistoric times. However, from an indigenous point of view, it must be remembered that when a Norseman said "one hundred" he had in mind 120 in our terms—therefore the formula from the "Grímnismál" would appear:

five hundred (= 600) and forty (40) = 640 (= 16 × 40)
eight hundred (= 960) (= 24 × 40)

and the multiplication of the two numbers would result in 614,400 (= 40 × 15,360). That two systemic key numbers (16 and 24) are present, and that there is an apparent instance of intentional multiples of forty, all seem to point to an independent and internally coherent Germanic number symbology. The final unlocking of this mystery is yet to come.

Runic Psychology

The lore of the soul—psycho-logy—is a complex but fundamental aspect of runic (esoteric) studies. The ancient Germanic peoples possessed a soul-lore as intricate and precise as any in history and far more complex than what we commonly have today. Much of this wondrous world can be recovered through the study of the words the ancients used to describe various soul conceptions and psychophysical processes. It is easy to see that when a group has a highly specialized or technical vocabulary in a given field it is because (1) they understand its intimate workings and need terms to distinguish various aspects of which they have knowledge, and (2) it is an area of life to which they attach a high level of importance. Besides the "souls," another idea that dominates Germanic thought is that of "fate"—wyrd. It cannot be fully understood apart from the lore of souls, and it helps to explain exactly *how* these souls are at work within us.

Forms of the Soul

It is somewhat of a misconception to separate a discussion of the "soul" from the "body" in runelore. They are intimately tied together, but, paradoxically, they may be consciously divided from one another through rune-work. Without such work this would naturally happen only at death. When speaking of the "whole person," it is perhaps most accurate to use the somewhat cumbersome terms psychophysical or psychosomatic (soul/body) complex. In any event, the soul is made up of various aspects—essences and/or substances that may lie more or less dormant in some individuals but in the runester are awakened to vital existence. It is hardly a wonder that once a people loses the terminology for an experience it soon fades from memory. Runelore and runework reawaken that memory.

Because the Norse were the last of the Germanic peoples to be "converted" to Christianity and because in Iceland the early phase of the conversion was of a tolerant nature, the Norse language and lore preserve intact the most complete runic psychology. It is on this lore that the following analysis is based. However, it appears most likely that all of the other Germanic peoples—Anglo-Saxons (English), Germans, Goths, and so on—had equivalent systems.

There are nine psychological constructs (each more or less complex) that go to make up the "whole man":

1. The physical vehicle is made up of several elements. The body itself (ON *lík*) is a complex of various substances (ON *efni*) such as "appearance" (a special ON term *lá* that may refer to the hair; also ON *sjón*, see *hamingja* below), movement (ON *læti*), health or good complexion (ON *litr*). These are the original gifts of the god Lódhurr. The "substances" of the body are gateways to other aspects of the self, and they are the ultimate receptacles of magical work. Therefore, certain subtle substances in the body become focal points for the development of the self or the person of whole consciousness, aware of all aspects in an exhalted ego state.

2. The "shape-substance" (ON *hamr*) is closely associated with the "body." It gives the plastic foundation or subtle matrix to physical reality. However, it can be brought under the control of the will (in the mind; ON *hugr*) and cause first subtle, then more substantial forms to take shape in accordance with the will. This is the power of imagination. Taken to its extreme forms it can cause "materializations" of imaginary beings (natural or non-natural) into which the consciousness can be projected. Old Norse literature is full of such descriptions. Most typically, the vitki lies as if asleep or dead, and in another location he is able to materialize an animal shape in which he can fight or stalk his enemy. If this shape is injured, the vitki will receive the wounds as well.

3. The faculty of ecstasy (ON *ódhr*) is the gift of the god Hœnir. This is as much an *experience*, a state of mind, as anything else. It is the faculty—

emotionally almost physically experienced—of rising up and out of the normal state of consciousness into a high level of energy and enthusiasm. *Óđhr* is the same root present in the name Óđh-inn, and it is by this power that magical force is manipulated. This is the active agent directed by the will. It is this power over which Óđhinn rules.

4. Closely linked with the ecstatic faculty is the vital breath (ON *önd*), which is the gift of Óđhinn. (It must be remembered that the triad Óđhinn-Hœnir-Lóđhurr actually represents a triform Óđhinn.) The *önd* is the "divine spark," the all-pervasive vital energy on which all life is based and which is the foundation of all runework. The concept is similar to the Indian *prāna*, and even the word itself is related to Sanskrit *ātman* (spirit, self). It is the bridge to higher levels of being.

5. The "mind" (ON *hugr*) is a complex entity indeed. It is actually made up of three faculties: (1) volition, (2) perception, and (3) cognition. This is the seat of the will, and as such it has the power to assimilate other aspects of the psychophysical complex to itself. This is why the term *hugr* is often used in Old Norse literature when other aspects might have been expected. It seems to "take over" the personalities of advanced runesters because their evolution comes more and more under conscious control. By this faculty, persons do analytical thinking of a conscious sort. It is synonymous with the left brain functions.

6. Intimately linked to the "mind" is the "memory" (ON *minni*). These are the two psychic aspects represented by Óđhinn's ravens: Huginn and Muninn (Mind and Memory). This faculty is indeed memory, but it is much more than what we commonly associate with this term. It is more than the simple recall of past events; it is the storehouse of all mysteries, the great rune-hoard. This is why, in the "Grímnismál" (st. 20), Óđhinn says of the relative values of Huginn and Muninn:

> The whole earth over,
> every day
> hover Huginn and Muninn;
> I dread lest Huginn
> droop in his flight,
> yet I fear me still more for Muninn.

A coordination of the mind and the memory faculties is what gives "intelligence." The mind processes external stimuli (including that received from memory), whereas memory (*minni*) *reflects* on its own infinite material. *Minni* is analogous to the right brain.

7. The "soul" (ON *sál*) usually comes into play only after death. This is the shade—a subtle body in which the psychic aspects (or some of them) are focused after the death of the physical aspects. In life this is the part of the psyche that passively receives the record of one's actions and remains the negative space into which one evolves. It is analogous to Jung's "shadow" concept of the unmanifested aspects of the psyche, discussed in the next section.

8. The "fetch" (ON *fylgja*) is in many respects the bright side of the shade. In men the fetch is seen as female, and in women it is male. Actually, there are three fetches, or "following spirits": in human form, in animal form, and in geometrical form. Each image has its own function. The one in human form is attached for the duration of life and can be passed on from generation to generation, either along genetic lines or according to willed projection. The animal-shaped fetch is usually in a form that corresponds to the character of the person to whom it is attached—a wolf, an eagle, a horse, a fox, a mouse, and so on. It can be separated from the vitki as a magical act. The vitki also may project his conscious will into the fetch in order to carry out magical workings. A geometrical shape is often seen by those with "second sight" going out *in front of* persons of great power. The *fylgja* is the repository of all of the actions of the persons to whom the entity was previously attached. It can be the source of great power but also of tremendous responsibilities and even hardships. This entity is the storehouse of *ørlög*—it can protect and it can doom. The fetch is closely related to, and in some cases identical to, the *valkyrja* or *dís* entity.

9. The "luck" (ON *hamingja*) of a person is extremely complex and in many ways closely linked to the fetch. *Hamingja*, which is linguistically derived from *hamr* (i.e., *ham-gengja*, one who can go about in another shape) is essentially a *power concept* analogous to Polynesian *mana*, Iroquois *orenda*, and so on. It too has some anthropomorphic symbols and is conceived of as (1) "luck" (personal power), (2) guardian spirit (symbolically derived from that luck), and (3) shape-shifting ability (which is its original meaning). A wide variety of consciously willed actions develop this magical power. It can be transferred from one person to another (although its effects are only temporary unless it is attached to the fetch-wife). The *hamingja* is the collective might and main of the individual. It is fed by and feeds the fetch-wife with power so that during a man's lifetime we can speak of a *hamingja–fylgja* complex that works in harmony.

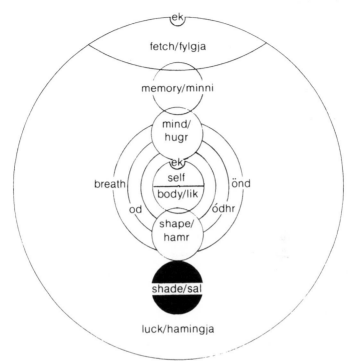

Figure 12.1. Germanic structure of the psychophysical complex

A schematic representation of the psychophysical complex (figure 12.1) perhaps gives a clearer image of just how these various concepts relate to and interact with one another. However, since the *reality* of this model, like that of Yggdrasill (figure 10.7 on page 154) is actually multi- or extradimensional, a two- or even three-dimensional model is somewhat inadequate.

Other structures that appear in the figure include the *ego*, or "I" concept and the magical "ego" (or *persona*). The "I" (ON *ek*) is linked to, or identical with, the *name* or names of the individual. On the Ódhinic path the runester—as he or she develops stronger links with the fetch and strengthens the powers of the other psychic aspects—forms magical "I" concepts allied with the fetch. These alternate personae are usually of the same gender as the "natural body." Each of the personae has a name and can be evoked with the right formula. It is in these self-shaped magical forms that the runester carries out rune workings. The magical personae can be quite numerous, but each embodies a part of the whole psychophysical complex; each is a hyper-aware entity. Ultimately, it is in these concepts that the essence of

Odianism is to be understood. This also gives a key to the understanding of Germanic heroic mythology, and each of the runestaves speak to at least one aspect of this realm.

Runic and Jungian Psychology

The only modern theoretical psychological structure that comes close to encompassing the power of the ancient Germanic practical soul-lore is that developed by the Swiss psychiatrist C. G. Jung. Jung's psychology has been the subject of "occult" investigations before, but the Germanic system seems unusually well suited to his structure because it is particularly understandable in Jungian terms. Jung himself devoted some space to the Wotan archetype in an article in which he compared the half-forgotten archetype to a dry riverbed that awaited only the release of the waters of life to renew it,

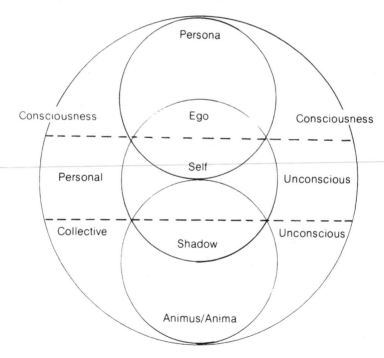

Figure 12.2. Jungian structure of the soul

along its old patterns. [1] So too it is with concepts of the soul. As a culture, we have been impoverished with regard to the soul—cut off from our ancestral ideas about it (or them)—and given only hazy, often contradictory doctrines as replacements. The time has now come that the waters of life be restored to their ancestral beds, and the souls will again come alive.

Jung's psychological scheme is characterized by certain structures, as figure 12.2 indicates. Jung's scheme, of course, lacks the overtly magical (practical) functions of the *hamingja-fylgja*, but their reflections remain in the process of the "alchemical marriage" between the animus and anima (the masculine and feminine sides of the soul). It is in the common process of a union between contrasexual aspects of the soul that the two systems are most alike on a practical level. Also, Jungian techniques designed to activate the "transcendent function" are of benefit in any effort to gain access to the fetch-wife or fetch of today.

In addition, the shadow bears a close resemblance to the "shade" function of the soul. Even gods have their shadows, for this is what Loki is to Óðhinn. Perhaps the most prominent feature of Jungian psychology is the structure of the collective unconscious. This comes as close as anything— perhaps with the addition of theories concerning the bihemispherical brain— to defining the true nature of *minni* and the mysteries taught by the raven Muninn.

[1] See C. G. Jung, "Wotan," in *Collected Works*, vol. 10 (tr. by R.F.C. Hull), (Princeton, NJ: Princeton University Press): 179–193.

Runelore of the Gods
(Esoteric Theology)

Runelore is dominated by the figure of Ódhinn. It is the path exemplified by
him that the runester seeks to travel. However, as Ódhinn has shown, other
gods are also essential for the healthy workings of the cosmological, sociological, and psychological orders. We know—from a tale told by the monk
Saxo Grammaticus in Book I of his *History of the Danes*—that it is the will of
Ódhinn to preserve and to promote the *whole* structure of the gods—the
entire pantheon. In this tale, we read that Ódhinn left his kingdom, and his
place was taken by one called Mitódhinn. The name Mitódhinn may mean
either "the one beside Ódhinn" (Mit-Ódhinn), or "the one who measures
out" (Mitódh-inn). In either case, it appears to be a name for Týr. Mitódhinn
tried to institute a separate cult for each of the gods. When Ódhinn returned,
he overthrew Mitódhinn and restored the common cult in which sacrifices
were made (three times a year) to *all* of the gods and goddesses of the
pantheon together. Mitódhinn's plan would certainly have led to fragmentation of the society, whereas Ódhinn's restoration was aimed at maintaining a
cohesive whole. As we will see, those two tendencies are what we should
expect of Ódhinn and Týr.

Before delving into the Ódhinic archetype we should, being true to the
Odian path, delineate the structure of the whole of the Germanic pantheon
from a runic or esoteric viewpoint. In the twentieth century two in-

vestigators, working from two different perspectives, have again provided keys with which to unlock the ways the divinities relate to each other. C. G. Jung, with his theory of archetypes within the collective unconscious (see chapter 12), has given a workable basis on which to understand the linkage between the human psyche and the gods and goddesses of our ancestors. Georges Dumézil, a French historian of religion and an Indo-Europeanist, has added the key to the structure of the pantheon.[1]

The gods and goddesses have both subjective (i.e., *within* the psyche of the individual) reality and a multiversal objective (i.e., *outside* the psyche of the individual) realities. These objective realities are essentially three: (1) within the national group (an inherited "metagenetic" divine pattern), (2) within the species *homo sapiens*, and (3) independent of humanity. Not all gods partake of all three objective realities. The first reality is the strongest objective link man can have with the divine. This metagenetic link is most powerful within close national/linguistic relationships, that is, ones that correspond to one's heritage (although all native English speakers will have absorbed a good deal of that nation's indigenous structures regardless of ethnic heritage). But "mega-nations" or linguistic groupings (e.g., Indo-European, Semitic, Sino-Tibetan) will have significant impact as well. Only Ódhinn, as the shaper of humanity, is independent of it.

What is a god or goddess? In runic terms a god is a living entity with some sort of existence independent of the individual psyche, although most gods may have had their ultimate origin there. It may be incorporated anywhere within the psychophysical complex; that is, it may have its origin in an instinctual, emotional, physical, mental, or spiritual pattern. A god, as most first perceive it, is a subtle tendency within the self, which then can be *fed* with psychic energy by means of myth, ritual, runework, and the like. The anthropomorphic shape of a god is a symbol. This is the simplest way for most people to grasp entities that have certain roles and complex inter-relationships. The anthropomorphic symbol is not altogether arbitrary because the gods are essentially creatures of the great force of consciousness given by the All-Father to *mankind* alone. A part of the god is housed within the *minni* of an individual and is inherited metagenetically from the ancestors.

In the final analysis, there are as many conceptions of the divine as there are individuals. No two persons comprehend a deity or theology in

---

[1] See Edred Thorsson, *Futhark: A Handbook of Rune Magic* (York Beach, ME: Samuel Weiser, 1984): 79.

exactly the same way, yet there are innate tendencies that are determined by living metagenetic forms. Of course, another method, used by the prophets of revealed religion, is that of dogma and coercion.

For the individual who may wish to understand the inner or outer reality of a god or goddess, a process of learning about the inner form and of linking that inner form with its external counterpart must be developed. This is a form of communication with the divinity and is a chief concern of *religion*. The task of the Odian runester goes somewhat beyond this, as we shall see.

The Great Gods of Æsir

The various Germanic divinities relate to one another in a way that is profound, archaic, and of great potency in the understanding of deep-level runelore. Table 13.1 on page 178 shows, in abbreviated form, the most important structural aspects of the oldest form of the Germanic pantheon. It amounts to a social structure of the pantheon and is essentially the Dumézilian restoration with additional runic insights.[2] On the other hand, the nonhuman elements of the multiverse extend beyond the realms of the Æsir and Vanir, and these worlds are represented in the pattern of Yggdrasill (refer to figure 10.7 on page 154).

Again, these relationships are to be found within individual psyches, within the national psyche of a people; they have their correspondences in the objective multiverse as well. To some extent these relationships give us the internal structure of the *minni*—the psychic "stuff" with which one is born. The dynamic interrelationships between these living inhabitants of this part of the psyche are the starting points for the great myths. Through various workings of a religious nature one may link the elements of one's own psyche with those in the objective world of the mythic tradition and become in-*formed* by them.

---

[2] See Edred Thorsson, *Futhark: A Handbook of Rune Magic* (York Beach, ME: Samuel Weiser, 1984): 79–80, and Georges Dumézil, *Gods of the Ancient Northmen* (ed. by E. Haugen) (Berkeley: University of California Press, 1973): 1–48.

Table 13.1. Structure of the Germanic Pantheon

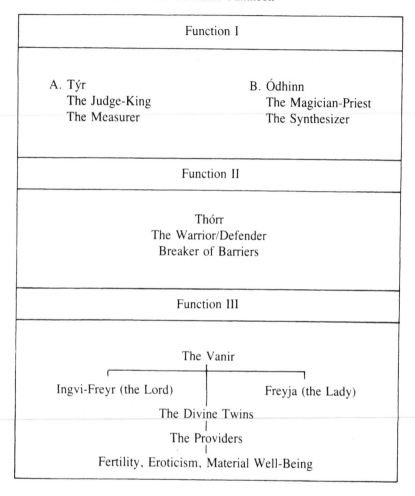

ÓDHINN

Although Ódhinn will be discussed in depth throughout this chapter, here we will put this divinity in the context of the whole pantheon.

Ódhinn is a god like no other. He is the Alfadhir—the All-Father. He is called this because he is the source of consciousness among the gods and mankind. His *gift* is the expanded human consciousness that allows the synthesizing self-concept to arise. It is for this reason that the active Odian does not so much seek to worship an external god-form of Óðhinn as he does him-*Self* to embody and to develop the Self-concept and consciousness given by *the god*. Whereas other religious cults turn outward to the objective manifestation of the particular god, the cult of Óðhinn turns inward and seeks a deification of the Self. The Odian does not worship his god—he becomes his god.

By his very nature Óðhinn *synthesizes* everything around him. He makes all things his own and uses them according to his *will*, while remaining in an essential way *apart* from outside things. In the history of Germanic myth, this can be seen as the Óðhinic archetype absorbs the Týric aspect and takes upon itself aspects of the warrior and craftsman/farmer.

The essential Óðhinic structure is threefold. The oldest name of this tripartite entity is *Wōdhanaz-Wiljōn-Wīhaz* (ON Óðhinn-Vili-Vé). The meanings of these names show us how this tripartite entity of consciousness works. *Wōdh-an-az* (master of inspiration [*wōdh-*]) is the expansive all-encompassing ecstatic and transformative force at the root of consciousness and enthusiasm. *Wiljōn* (the will) is the conscious application of a desired plan consciously arrived at, and *Wīhaz* (the sacred) is the spirit of *separation* in an independent sacred "space." This separation between consciousness and "nature" (that outside consciousness) must be effected before any transformations or "work" can take place. All three are necessary; all three should work together as a whole.

Although Óðhinn is first and foremost the god of synthetic consciousness, this characteristic allowed him to assume the roles of the god of the dead, of poetry, and of intellectual crafts of all kinds (including runes). This latter aspect made him the favorite of the elite bands of innovative and aware warriors and kings.

Essential to the Óðhinic mystery is his manifold nature. He is the whole made up of many parts. In the mythology this is made clear not only by his tripartite appearances but also by his many "nicknames" (ON *heiti*). More than a hundred of these have been documented. A litany of a substantial number of them can be found in the "Grímnismál" (sts. 47–55). These range from names meaning Worker of Evil (ON *Bölverkr*) to Father of All (ON *Alföðhr*) and every quality in between. Perhaps one of the names sums up this quality—*Svipall* (the Changeable One), which indicates the ultimate transformational character of the god. This divine case of "multiple personalities" gives an indication as to why Óðhinn is often misunderstood. Indeed, those who approach him from a non-Odian viewpoint will be disappointed, confused, or destroyed.

If the *heiti* were not enough to confuse the noninitiate, the greater aspects (hypostases) have even confounded many experts. A hypostasis is an aspect of a god that *seems* to be an independent god-form but on closer investigation is shown to be a particularly well-developed functional aspect of it. Because of his many-sided character, Ódhinn is especially subject to this mode of understanding. Figure 13.1 shows the eight great hypostases of Ódhinn. Some of these are dual in nature.

Vili and Vé have been discussed and will be explained further in the "Ódhinn: The Hidden God of the Runes" section below. The forms Lódhurr and Hœnir are Ódhinn's counterparts in the anthropogonic myth reported by Snorri in his *Prose Edda*. Hœnir also figures as a partner with another god named Mímir. When these two god-forms were given as hostages to the Vanir at the conclusion of the First War, Hœnir, who was reputed to be wise, proved to be "empty-headed" unless advised by Mímir. This so angered the Vanir that they cut off Mímir's head and sent it back to the Æsir. Ódhinn is said to preserve the head in order to learn hidden lore from it. At first glance this myth is baffling, especially when we see that Hœnir is otherwise depicted as a powerful intellectual force. In the "Völuspá" he gives Askr and Embla *ódhr*, and after Ragnarök he comes back as the chief diviner of the

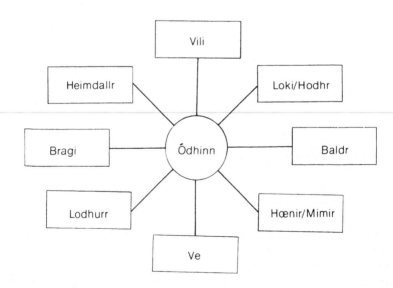

Figure 13.1. The eight great aspects of Ódhinn

gods who can read the runestaves. But everything becomes clear when Hœnir/Mímir are understood as aspects of Óðhinn. The fact that they never really act independently is one indication of this, but their *names* contain the key. Hœnir is derived from the same root as *hugr*, and Mímir is related to the same root as *minni*. Therefore, we have figures related to Óðhinn in the same way as their zoomorphic counterparts Huginn and Muninn, the ravens of Óðhinn. These are the cognitive and reflective functions of the god.

Bragi is the poetic aspect of the god and a name taken by an ancient skald who became identified with the elder god of poetry. Baldr is the young warrior aspect of Óðhinn and also an aspect that relates to the initiation of the young warrior into the band of armed men. Heimdallr is the guardian aspect of Óðhinn. He guards the Rainbow Bridge (Bifröst) against the coming of the rime-thurses, but he is also the aspect that continually communicates with mankind. It is Óðhinn, in the form of Heimdallr and going by the nickname Rígr, that becomes the progenator of human society. The mystery of Heimdallr is found in the M-rune.

The most puzzling hypostasis of all is that of Loki. In Loki, Óðhinn contains the seed of his own destruction but also a necessary part of the process of his rebirth and transformation in the new age. Loki, as a name and as a separate entity, is a latecomer to the Germanic pantheon and is really found only in sources of Norse origin. But in most respects the characteristics of Loki correspond to the "darker" one of Óðhinn as the sly, deceitful, perverse god. In a way, Loki is the objectified shadow-self of Óðhinn. But he still works together with his "dark brother," and it is even said that they become "blood brothers" see "Lokasenna," st. 9). Actually, they are of the same "blood."

Where Loki is most conspicuous is in his role connected to Ragnarök— the Judgment of the Gods. Once one realizes that the Ragnarök process is actually a model of transformation and that the central triadic figures of Óðhinn-Baldr-Loki/Höðr can be understood as internal forces, the true meaning of the "dark brother" becomes clearer. The blind Höðr (whose name means "warrior") is guided by the force of negation (Loki) to kill the Lord of Light, the bold Baldr (another name meaning "warrior"). Baldr is sent to the dark, still enclosure of Hel, informed by the greatest of secrets (runes) that Óðhinn whispered into his ear as he was on the pyre before being sent Hel-ward. There he awaits Ragnarök to be reborn in the new age. Loki too is cast down and bound in the underworld as punishment for his murderous act. There he too awaits the "final conflict." This deed of the dark blood brother has set the process toward Ragnarök in motion. When the final hour comes, Ódhinn, with his hosts of Valhöll and Ásgardhr turn southward to face Loki and the forces of Hel and Muspellsheimr. The god of consciousness has turned to face his shadow-self. Heimdallr and Loki kill one another, and Ódhinn is swallowed by the Fenris-Wolf (a son of Loki). In turn, Ódhinn is avenged by his son Vídharr, who kills the Wolf by either splitting him open with a sword or ripping his jaws apart. Rune wisdom tells us that this means Ódhinn too is "reborn," in a transformed state, into the new age. But in what form? He is Hœnir made whole, who will "handle the blood-twigs."

When viewed as a mythic paradigm of transformation, the Ragnarök process takes on meanings that are powerful and useful in runework, and it gives a deeper understanding of the function of Loki and of Ódhinn's "dark side."

Before returning to Ódhinn's meaning and might, we should explore the ways that the Odian views the other holy gods of the North.

TÝR

The essential mysteries of this god are embodied in the T-rune that is named after him. Týr is the god of justice and of self-sacrifice for the good of society. This aspect is illustrated by the myth in which the gods capture the Fenris-Wolf by binding him with a fetter made of six things that indicate subtle mysteries, while Týr holds his (right) hand in the jaws of the Wolf as a pledge of troth. When Fenrir finds he cannot escape, Týr's hand is sacrificed to the jaws of the son of Loki (the Wolf). As a mythic figure, Týr retreats into the realm of relative inactivity after this. However, in religious practice (especially that connected to *legal* matters) he remains a god of great importance. *Tues*day is named after him. In German we have *Dienstag* which is derived from an older form *Dings-tag*, day of the *thing* (legal assembly). So in one language we have the god; in the other we have the instruction over which he ruled.

As the overall structure of the psychocosmological aspects of the pantheon shows, ideally Týr and Ódhinn should work together in harmony as the left brain and right brain, respectively. In the process of shaping or creating anything, both forces are necessary. The Týr aspect lays the plans, and the Ódhinic aspect puts the plans into action and makes them real. Týr is the planner; Ódhinn, the doer. The Germanic soul is essentially one of action and eternal motion. For this reason the Ódhinic aspect was always at least slightly dominant in the pantheon; Ódhinn is the high god and the All-Father. Ódhinn's expansive transformational essence led to his aspect, largely synthesizing that of Týr. Nowhere is this clearer than in the later legendary name of the North Star, Ódhinn's Eye. The North Star is, of course, primarily identified with Týr (see the T-rune), but in a sense Týr becomes the all-seeing eye of Ódhinn aloft on Hlidhskjálf, the Gate-Tower. This is the eye that sees all over the worlds, whereas that which is pledged in Mimir's Well is the eye that sees "beneath" all the worlds, into their deepest secrets (runes).

The latent antagonism between Ódhinn and Týr is merely that which often occurs within systems composed of complementary aspects. An act of will is needed to cause them to work together harmoniously.

THÓRR

This god seems simple, yet he is complex. Great mysteries of Thórr are contained in the TH-rune. Essentially, Thórr is the ancient god of war. In later times, as Ódhinn absorbed that function, he lost much of that attribute among men. Yet we note that he retains it among the gods themselves. He is their defender and the one who exercises his brute strength and power of his cosmic hammer, Mjöllnir, against the nonconscious or preconscious forces of Jötunheimr.

The Æsir—gods of ancestral consciousness and transformation—are faced with the forces of nonconsciousness and entropy pressing in from the east and south—out of Útgardhr. To oppose these forces the gods need a power very similar to that of the thurses and etins but loyal to them alone. This is Thórr. Thórr does little "thinking" for himself; he follows the orders given by the sovereign gods. Realistically speaking, there is, of course, superficial antagonism between the "Warrior" and the "Wizard" (see the "Harbardhsljódh" in the *Poetic Edda*), but ultimately the Warrior follows the guidance of the Wizard. The Wizard rules by wisdom; the Warrior rules by weapons. As long as Ódhinn remains dominant, wisdom rules the weapon. It is Thórr out of balance that leads to national catastrophe.

FREYJA

Although the "theology" of runic practice is dominated by Ódhinn as the great runemaster, another figure—Freyja—looms large in the practice of Germanic magic. She is even said to have taught Ódhinn a form of magic known in Old Norse as *seidhr* (shamanistic trance-inducing methods). In many ways Freyja is the female counterpart of Ódhinn. She is the magical archetype for women involved in magical pursuits, as Ódhinn is for men. In her most basic aspects, Freyja is "the Lady" (this is the literal meaning of her name). Her companion is her brother/lover Freyr, "the Lord." However, it would be a large mistake, as we have already noted, to assume that Freyja is primarily a fertility goddess. Among the Vanir, it must be remembered, she is the one chiefly concerned with the numinous. In her very essence she embodies a profound relationship to the Odian pathways.

Like Ódhinn, Freyja is known by many names. Some examples of these are Vanadís (the Goddess of the Vanir), Vanabrúdhr (Bride of the Vanir), Hörn (Mistress of Flax), Gefn (the Giver), Sýr (the Sow—her solar aspect), Mardöll (the Sea-bright), and Gullveig (Gold-Greedy). These names tell us quite a bit about the range of Freyja's functions and her position. She is of great importance among the Vanir, perhaps in many places superior to her brother. She is indeed connected with prosperity and growth, and she gives her gifts (material and numinous) to humans. In her cosmic aspect she is connected to the sun (which is feminine in Germanic; see the S-rune) through her image as the "golden sow." The boar and sow are the animals of Freyr and Freyja, respectively. In Germany today, when the sun is very hot, they still say *Die gelbe Sau brennt* (The yellow sow is burning). The linkage with gold is made on many occasions, and on one level this is a further expression of Freyja's capacity as Vanic deity of prosperity and well-being. There is another level that is made clear in the mystery of *fehu*.

In the "Völuspá" we read how a certain sorceress named Gullveig came to the Æsir from the Vanir when those two groups of gods were at war. This is Freyja in another guise. We know this because, although Freyja is later found among the Æsir, she is *not* one of the Vanir (Freyr, Njördhr, and perhaps also Kvasir) who went over to the Æsir as hostages as a part of the truce between the two divine races.

Before we consider three of Freyja's myths in some detail, it might be well to remember how much of her lore is lost. At one time there was a vast body of mythic and cultic material connected with the goddess, but perhaps because of the often *erotic* nature of her mysteries and myths they were especially singled out for eradication by the monkish missionaries to the north. Even in normally tolerant Iceland, her poetry—the *mansöngr* (love song)—was prohibited. Unfortunately also, her cult could not recede into the protective confines of the chieftain's hall. But some of it was saved by the skald's art.

Heidh

During the First War—the war between the Æsir (first and second functions) and the (third function) Vanir—a sorceress named Gullveig came to the

Æsir, into Ódhinn's hall. The Æsir tried to kill her by piercing her with spears and burning her. But each time she was reborn. The third time she transformed herself from Gullveig into Heidh (the Shining One). This "thrice-born" *völva* (seeress) is certainly Freyja, and it is in this form that she became Ódhinn's teacher in the ways of *seidhr*. After her lore and her cult had been assimilated into that of Ódhinn and of the Æsir, the lore of *seidhr* became an integral (but specialized) field within runelore (in the sense of esoteric studies).

Brisingamen

The necklace of the Brisings is much more than a pretty trinket. It is the all-encompassing fourfold cosmic ring, under the control of the great goddess Freyja. It is the magical equivalent of the Midhgardh-Serpent that girdles the entire cosmos. The *Tale of Sörli* tells us how Freyja obtained this magical tool by spending a night with each of the four dwarves—the Brisings (descendants of the Shining Ones)—who forged the necklace. These four dwarves may be the same as Nordhri, Austri, Sudhri, and Vestri, who are stationed at the four cardinal directions of the world. It may have originally been that she had sexual relations with all four, simultaneously or over four nights. In any event, the result is the same: Freyja gains control over the fourfold cycle of the cosmos and its generative and regenerative powers. The object is said to be worn either as a belt or as a necklace, depending on how the goddess wished to use its power. At one point the mischievous god Loki stole the Brisinga-men from Freyja, and it was restored to her only after it had been recovered by the god Heimdallr. What is interesting here is that both Loki and Heimdallr are considered aspects (hypostases) of Ódhinn—his dark and light sides if you will.

Search for Ódhr

It is said that Freyja is married to a god named Ódhr, who is none other than Ódh-inn himself. The name Ódh-r simply indicates the force of ecstasy, of the magically inspired mind. To this, indeed, the goddess Freyja is wedded, and it too (as with Ódhinn himself) is the chief aim of her strivings. As Ódhr wandered, so Freyja wandered after him, shedding tears of gold. Many have wanted to see in this mournful search a parallel with the search of Ishtar for Tammuz. However, the significance of this Sumerian/Akkadian myth and that of Freyja's search for Ódhr is quite different. Freyja's quest has nothing directly to do with fertility—she is seeking the "numinous inspiration" embodied in the god.

Each of these three myths indicates something of Freyja's primarily magical or numinous character. That fertility, wealth, well-being, and eroticism grow out of this character is perhaps secondary but nevertheless essential.

Another important fact about Freyja is that she receives one-half of all those slain in battle, according to her choice, to go to her otherworldly stonghold called Folkvangr (Field of the Warrior-band). The other half, of course, goes to Ódhinn.

Like Ódhinn, Freyja is a threefold divinity. She, as no other goddess is able to do, covers all three functions of the pantheon: (1) she is a magical figure, (2) she is a goddess of warriors, and (3) she is a Vanic deity with all the powers of that race of gods. She can bring things into being, can cause them to become, and can cause them to pass away toward new beginning. This magical power is at the root of her fertility function. Ultimately, the "marriage" between Freyja and Ódhinn is a rather "modern" one. Freyja is *not* the "feminine side" of Ódhinn (he carries that comfortable within himself—or in his "devilish" aspect, Loki); nor is Ódhinn the "masculine side" of the Lady—she contains this as well. Perhaps Freyr even originally grew out of Freyja the way the masculine Njördhr grew out of the feminine Nerthus. In any case, we are dealing with two individuated deities drawn together by a common purpose. There are still a great many mysteries to be unraveled about this most powerful of goddesses.

FREYR

Of all the gods, the one most independent of Ódhinn is Freyr, the God of This World (ON *veraldar godh*). Despite this independence, or perhaps because of it, there is little conflict between the Lord and Ódhinn. In fact, it seems they *secretly* conspire with one another in many regards. Through runic investigation we find that besides Ódhinn it is Freyr who is best represented in the ancient runelore. By this fact the runesters of old acknowledge the importance of the Lord in the workings of the world.

Freyr is not the god's actual name but a title. This is not unusual. But in this case we perhaps have the actual name of the god in the name of the NG-rune: *Ingwaz*. It is also possible that two gods are assimilated here, as the originally Æsiric Ing and the Vanic Freyr. The mysteries of the god are contained in the NG-rune. Yngvi is also a great progenitor of royal houses (especially in Sweden); the Ynglings are the greatest clan of the Sviar (Swedes).

Although Freyr is sometimes connected to the imagery of war, he is most often a figure of peace, prosperity, and pleasure. At Midsummer the

Norse sacrificed to him for good harvest and peace (ON *til árs ok fridhar*). Another name of Freyr is perhaps Fródhi, who in the form of a legendary king ruled over a golden age of peace in the north called *Fródha fridhr* (Peace of Fródhi). Runically, all of this points us in the direction of *jera* (younger name, *ár*). Remember that for *ár* the "Old Norwegian Rune Rhyme" reads: "I say that Fródhi was generous." In Freyr, the Lord of the World, we see the force ruling over the organic processes that bind together the J- and NG-runes. The : ⋄ : is the closed circle of the year, the cycle of gestation, and : ⧓ : is the dynamic opening of the yearly cycle at harvest when the fruit is born forth.

Ódhinn and Freyr work most harmoniously together in the *Völsunga Saga*. Yet this cooperation is largely hidden from the uninitiated eye. That Ódhinn is the divine progenitor of the Völsungs and that he and his agents are responsible for the initiation of the members of this clan into the secrets of the gods is well known and obvious. But in his little-expressed warrior aspect Freyr is also present in the greatest of the Völsungs—Sigurdhr (or Siegfried) the Dragon-Slayer. In some versions of his myth Sigurdhr is raised by hinds in the woods and is later identified as a hart (which is his animal-fetch). Now Freyr is also closely associated with this high-horned beast, and after giving up his sword to gain the favor of the etin-wife, Gerdhr, he must fight with all that is left to him—the horn of a stag. This and other hidden associations show us that Freyr and Ódhinn could work together in an independent fashion to form great initiates—Ódhinn as progenitor and initiatory sponsor and Freyr as earthly provider.

Wights

Besides the high gods—Æsir and Vanir—there are a number of important beings that inhabit other dewllings in other worlds within the branches of Yggdrasill. Ódhinn actively and fruitfully interacts with beings in all of these worlds. Ódhinn himself is, after all, a synthesis of the pure streams of thurs-force and god-consciousness (see chapter 10), and his inherently expansive consciousness seeks wisdom in all realms and rejects nothing that might be instrumental in effecting his will.

ELVES

The elves (ON *álfar*; sg., *álfr*) are a complex lot. They dwell in (Ljóss)ál-
fheimr and are sometimes associated with Freyr. The word elf means "the
shining-white one." These are entities of light (not always seen because
exceedingly small in stature) that sometimes interact beneficially and sometimes maliciously with humans. Essentially, they are the collective light-
bodies or "minds" (ON *hugar*) of the ancestors (in their female forms they
are called *dísir* or dises or ides) that continue to have contact with the minds
of humans. They have much lore and wisdom to teach. They are the mental
faculties of the ancestors that have been reabsorbed into the cosmic organism.

DWARVES

The dwarves are also known in Old Norse as *svart-* or *dökk-álfar*, and they
dwell "below" Midhgardhr in Svartalfheimr. These entities too have much
lore to teach, but their main function is that of *formulators*. They are the
shapers of shapes that come into being in Midhgardhr, especially those
shapes capable of effecting the will of a great warrior or magician. That is
why they are always said to be the forgers of magical weapons. They also can
be considered the reabsorbed ancestral skills and crafts.

RISES–ETINS–THURSES

The words most often translated simply "giant" are actually three different
words in the tradition. Old Norse *rísi* (ris) is a true *giant*, an entity of great
size and perhaps even ultimately referring to the prehistoric inhabitants of
the north. They are often said to intermarry with humans and to bear children
with them. In addition, they are more often than not beneficent and often
beautiful to look at. The etins (ON *jötnar*, sg. *jötunn*) are characterized by
great strength and age, although size is not of particular importance. They
can be vast as the worlds (Ymir) or virtually microscopic (the name of a
certain beetle in Old Norse is *jötunuxi* [etin-ox]). Etins are vastly potent
ageless entities who often contain the wisdom of the aeons through which
they have existed. In regard to the eternal "battle" between the conscious and
nonconscious, they are neutral. That is, some side with the Æsir and some
with the thurses. What is certain is that they *are*. Etins are nonevolving
beings—they are now as they were in aeons past. It is for this reason that
Ódhinn often engenders children with etin-wives. The forces of

nonconsciousness are embodied in the thurses (ON *thursar*, sg., *thurs*). They are, even in later tales, marked by their *stupidity*. Thurses too are of great age (see chapter 10), but they are actively antagonistic toward the forces of consciousness and seek to destroy it through their rime-cold entropy. The "sons of Muspell"—and their leader, Surt—who come out of Muspellsheimr to destroy cosmic order with fire also may be ascribed to this group—the polar opposites of the rime-thurses. It is impossible, from a Odian point of view, to call these forces "evil"; they are merely nonconscious natural forces of the mechanical or organic multiverse that eternally seek stasis.

The lore of all of the gods and all of the wights throughout the multiverse is to be mastered by the Odian. Therefore, nothing lies outside his interest, and no path is closed to him. But before the ways of other gods are opened to the Odian, the deep essence of the road shown by the great god must be fathomed.

Ódhinn: The Hidden God of the Runes

Ódhinn must be known forever in his true nature as the *omnideus*, the whole-god of inner being/transformation and timeless mystery. Ódhinn holds the holy words to open the doors of the new dawn, but he will not give them away; we must win them by our own wills. To do this the first step is the discovery of the character of his godhood.

What is meant by the formulation "Ódhinn: Hidden God of the Runes"? First of all, let us restate and expand the etymology of the name Ódhinn. The name occurs in most of the major Germanic dialects (OHG *Wuotan*, OE *Wōden*, as well as ON *Ódhinn*). The Germanic form of the name would have been *Wōdhanaz*, which is quite transparent in meaning. *Wōdh-* is a term for ecstatic, inspired numinous or mental activity; it is almost like a physiological response in the psychophysical complex to a high level of stimulation present in such phenomena as ecstasy, enthusiasm, outflowings of physical power, and the feeling of awe in the presence of the *numinosum tremendum* (the terrifying aspect of the "divine"). *Wōdh* is first and foremost a magical power concept. The element *-an-* regularly indicates the "master of" whatever concept it is attached to. (Other examples of this would be Old Norse *thjódh-inn*, the master of the people (= king), and Old Norse *drótt-inn*, the master of the warrior band. The grammatical ending *-az-* is already familiar to the reader from the rune names. In most cases this ending became an *-r* in Old Norse, but following an *-n-* it changed to an *-n* as well. Also, the loss of initial *w-* before a long *ó* or *ú* is already known from the relationship between Old Norse *Urdhr* and Old English *Wyrd*. Thus, *Ódhinn* is just a regular development from *Wodhanaz*.

The Master of Inspiration is only one of many characterizing names (*heiti*) ascribed to this age-old and actually nameless, hidden god. The esoteric numen or archetype of the mysteries is not hidden by a veil as such, nor is it mainly occulted by its transcendence alone but rather by its omnipresence. That is the key to his many names. What makes Ódhinn especially "occult" is his intense presence in paradoxical formulations. His co-equal presence as a binding force between opposites is an essential feature of his character, yet one that often baffles the human view that tends to understand things in a more dualistic–analytical way. But Ódhinn comprehends through the whole entity expressed by polar constructs. Ódhinn sees with the whole eye. This is the essence that hides him from our rational ("two-eyed") minds—he is the embodiment of the "suprarational-all."

Ódhinn is a god because he serves (and has served for aeons) as an exemplary model for the expression, development, and transformation of human consciousness. This was for long ages institutionalized in a "national cultus" among the Germanic peoples, with each tribe holding its special versions of emphasis within a general traditional framework. Ódhinn, by any name, served this function since the birth of Indo-European humanity, and hence cannot be extinguished except through the physical destruction of his people.

The runes are an integral part of the Odhinic essence because it is through them and by them that he grows in power, becomes indestructible, and is able to communicate multiversal mysteries to his human kindred. Ódhinn, the runes, and humanity form a matrix in which the conscious/unconscious and existence/nonexistence meet.

To establish a traditional framework for the exploration and emulation of the Ódhinic archetype, it is wise to read what was composed about Ódhinn's evolution in the nights when his ways were an established, institutionalized life-style, uncluttered by centuries of intervening ignorance. For this we must concentrate on the sources of Ódhinn's wisdom and power as outlined in passages in Old Norse literature.

The primary Ódhinic initiatory myth is that of the self-sacrifice on Yggdrasill described in the "Hávamál," stanzas 138 to 165. This process must be understood as taking place in a realm beyond time, in that immense cosmogonic space before the advent of the Nornic Laws (see the N- and P-runes). The "birth" of Ódhinn and the World-Tree self-sacrifice are essentially simultaneous—without it Ódhinn is not Ódhinn. In this process Ódhinn gives his *self* to him-*Self* while hanging on Yggdrasill (the steed of Yggr [= Ódhinn], or the yew-column). The subject has turned upon itself and has successfully made itself the object of its own work. Ódhinn becomes omnijective. In this action Ódhinn meets with the dark realm of Hel—the unconscious—and merges with it *while keeping his wits*. Thus, in a flash of inspiration he is infused with the entirety of the runic pattern. Because Ódhinn is, by his tripartite essence, a conscious entity, this pattern is reshaped by his will into a *communicable* form. Through this central Ódhinic mystery the conscious is melded with the unconscious, the light with the dark, and it is made comprehensible by the supraconscious essence of Ódhinn. The runes then begin to be formulated by Ódhinn into a metalanguage contained in the runic system, in poetry, and in natural language, as "one word leads to another, and one work leads to another." The seed of Ódhinn, his gift, is then the essence that makes this comprehension possible in his descendants: conscious humanity.

A complex source of Ódhinn's secret wisdom is found in Mímir. As we have seen (page 180), Mímir is really the "memory" aspect of Ódhinn and a counterpart to the Hœnir aspect. Mímir belongs, even on the exoteric level, to that generation of "first Æsir" sometimes identified as a wise Ase, sometimes as an etin. This twofold nature is due to the fact that Mímir is to a large extent the "ancestral memories" of Ódhinn, whose ancestors are among the thurses and etins! Ódhinn derives wisdom from this aspect in two ways: (1) from the severed head of Mímir and (2) from his eye, which he has hidden or pledged to Mímir's Well.

From the myth of the hostage exchange between the warring Æsir and Vanir (see page 180) we learned that Mímir's head was cut off by the angry Vanir because they felt cheated that Hœnir (Mímir's partner) was less intelligent than he had been represented to be. Ódhinn preserved this head in herbs and spoke spells over it to keep it alive. It is kept, with older wisdom, at Mímir's Well. The consultation with the "head of Mímir" is then a magical image in which the self is shown to have access to the *minni* aspect. But because it has been "severed" due to mistrust of it by noninitiates, it

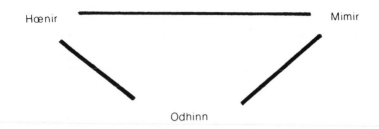

Figure 13.2. Ódhinn-Hœnir-Mímir complex

requires magical acts of will to keep the channels of communication open to it. When Ódhinn gets rede from Mímir's head (memory), Hœnir (mind) is informed, and thus another threefold pattern is completed as shown in figure 13.2. Ultimately, "Mímir's head" is a metaphor that indicates the focusing of consciousness in the *minni*—in the Well of Mímir.

This Well of Mímir is said to be under a root of Yggdrasill (also called in ON *Mímameith* [Mímir's Tree]) that is over Jötunheimr. In order to gain and grow in wisdom, Ódhinn desires to drink of the waters of this well, but Mímir's head asks of him one of his eyes—a part of himself—as a pledge or sacrifice. Ódhinn "hides" his eye down in the column of vertical consciousness, down in the depths. There his eye remains active, always able to see, to "drink in," the wisdom of all the worlds. Thus, Ódhinn always has *two* visions—one over "this world" (from Hlidhskjálf) and one in the "other worlds" (from the Well of Mímir). It also might be pointed out that Heimdallr also stores his *hljódh* (hearing, or ear) at this well; thus, he (Ódhinn) is also able to hear in all the worlds.

In the myth of Mímir, the Odian recognizes the necessity for access to the realm of *minni*, the inherited storehouse of magico-mythic imagery, and the necessity for a synthesis of the various psychic aspects designated by the names Mímir and Hœnir. This is done through a magical act of will by means of a secret "technology" whereby the focal point (head) of this storehouse is obtained, preserved, and assimilated. One eye is focused downward into the well of "wyrd" (images), and the other is focused outward into the wide worlds of words and works. (Again the functions of the bihemispherical brain seem indicated.)

Ódhinn also gains knowledge from sources outside himself. The main source of this kind is Freyja. As we have seen, the Vanadis taught Ódhinn the arts of *seidhr*. There is every reason to believe that this took place in some sort of sexual initiatory context in which certain secrets of what might today be called "sex magic" were originally passed from female initiates to males and from male initiates to females. In myth we see this reflected in the magical marriages between a warrior and his valkyrie or between humans and superhuman initiators. The "Rúnatals tháttr Ódhins" (see page 105) tells us that the eighteenth secret (probably here to be ascribed to the G-rune) is spoken to no one "except her who embraces me or who is my sister." It is in this cultic context that Ódhinn and Freyja exchange occult secrets. The techniques of *seidhr* include trance induction for divinatory purposes, shape shifting (which also can be done with *galdr*), the deprivation of others' souls, creation of illusions, and other arts more or less shamanistic. These techniques were often used in aggressive magic, which in part has led to its being thought of as evil magic. But perhaps another trait led to its reputation as being "unmanly"; that is the practice of men transforming themselves into women in order to engender magical beings (often harmful ones) through sexual sorcery. In this fashion Loki becomes the mother of the steed Sleipnir.

Another of these quests assumes an importance second only to the Yggdrasill rite: the winning of the poetic mead from the realm of the etins. The poetic mead had been created from the blood of Kvasir, who was a linking being between the Æsir and Vanir when they made their truce. (In one version of the myth he is shaped from the spittle of the two divine races; in another he is simply one of the Vanir sent as hostage [see the *Skaldskaparmál* in the *Prose Edda*, chapter 1]). In any case, Kvasir was reputed to be the "wisest of all beings," but he is killed by some dwarves, who make the poetic mead from his blood. This liquid—the essence of the inspired consciousness of the Æsir and the organic unconscious of the Vanir—eventually came into the possession of the etins (by nature beings of the nonconscious realm). Therefore, the mead by necessity had to be won back by Ódhinn "by hook or crook." This myth is described both by Snorri (*Skaldskaparmál*, chapter 1) and in the "Hávamál" (sts. 104–110). The process by which this is done is most significant. In the guise of Bölverkr (Worker of Evil) and by cunning and oath-breaking, he gains access to the mountain (*Hnitbjörg*—knit-mountain), where an etin-wife, Gunnlödh, guards the mead. He bores his way into the mountain in the shape of a serpent and remains in the interior for three nights, sleeping with the etin, after which he gets to drink down the mead in three gulps from the three vessels—Ódhrœrir, Són, and Bodhn—in which the mead was held. Then he shape-shifts into an eagle and flies out of the top of the mountain and back to Ásgardhr, where he spits out the mead

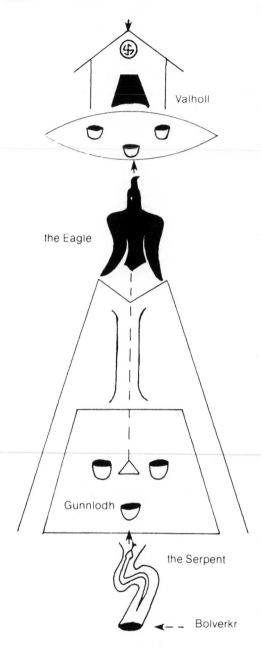

Figure 13.3. The rewinning of the poetic mead

into three vats—thus returning the mead to its rightful place among the Æsir and humanity. It is specifically stated that some of the mead dropped to the earth when Ódhinn flew away, and this *anyone* can drink (if he or she happens upon it be accident). Thus, it is called the "fool-poet's share."

This myth is vital to the runic tradition. The sign of the Rune-Gild— three interlocked drinking horns—is derived from this tale. It describes the path of becoming, the pathway of transformational Odianism, and the essential mission of the Gild: to serve the larger conscious community of gods and men.

Figure 13.3 graphically shows the process of the rewinning of the of the poetic mead of inspiration. In this process we see the amoral force of Ódhinn, obeying only his higher laws of will and service to the path of becoming/consciousness, gain access to the hidden realm that conceals the ill-gotten power by transforming himself into a serpent. He allies himself with the underworldly forces of dissolution to break through the mountain and to enable himself to traverse the exceedingly narrow etin-ways of dense reality. Here is hidden the significance of the serpentine aspect of the Ódhinic cult, well known from snake-bands on runestones and the famous dragon ships of the Vikings. While in the interior chamber with Gunnlödh— perhaps in conjunction with rites of sexual sorcery in which darkness and light are wedded (knit together; see the meaning of the name of the mountain)—Ódhinn consumes all the mead from the three vats. The static force of the mead held by the etins, but useless to them, is now reassimilated to Ódhinn who transforms himself into an eagle, the wide-ranging bird of prey that transmits the ecstatic force back to the world of the Æsir, separate from the world of men and under the control of consciousness. There the mead is rearticulated into its threefold essence and returned to the three vessels: (1) Ódhrœrir (the exciter of inspiration, which is also a name of the mead itself), (2) Són (atonement), and (3) Bodhn (container). The significance in the number of these vessels is in the threefold essence of the mead itself. Normally, this "triessence" of consciousness is only shared by Ódhinn with the Æsir and with human initiates of his cult.

The path of the serpent leads to wisdom (: ᚺ :). In the mountain enclosure (: ᛒ :) opposites are wed (: ᛗ :) and inspiration is gained (: ᚠ :), to be returned by the flight of the eagle (: ᚲ :) to the enclosure of the gods and initiates (: ᛉ :), to be given (: ᚷ :) by the great god to those in his band. In this myth we see why Ódhinn is considered both the Drighten of Darkness and the Lord of Light.

Ódhinn's wisdom is derived from three continuous sources: (1) the Yggdrasill sacrifice (for rune wisdom), (2) Mímir's Well (the head of Mímir and the "hidden eye"), and (3) the poetic mead (Ódhrœrir). The mythic paradigms connected to these sources give shape to the process of the acquisition of runelore, rune wisdom, and runecraft. They also serve as psychic models that the runester follows in the Ódhinic pattern. The "god" Ódhinn is on one level something separate from the paradigm of "that which comprehends opposites" at the root of the Ódhinic mystery. These aspects can be contained in the archetype concept (if not in the strictest Jungian terms). The archetype is not a personified thing but rather an impersonal pattern of action or pure consciousness. As this paradigm becomes more conscious in the human being, a "personification" of that pattern begins to emerge and to act as an exemplary model of consciousness and behavior—a "god." From the Odian point of view this is the process of all gods and goddesses.

Here we want to concentrate on Ódhinn the god as a psychic model for the evolution of the runemaster, the role of the runes and their interaction with and assimilation to this model, and why Ódhinn must ever remain the hidden god.

At the root of the Ódhinic archetype is the concept of wholeness within twofoldness. His origins show this quite clearly. He is born of Borr, son of Búri (of the race of proto-gods) and Bestla, daughter of the etin Bölthorn. Ódhinn therefore represents a synthesis of the primal (preconscious) entities (see chapter 10). The bridging function is something that he eventually can give to his human kindred.

From this twofoldness comes the great manifoldness ("all-ness") that is represented throughout the Ódhinic literature by his unlimited names and shapes. This manifold character is most formally represented in Ódhinn's all-pervasive number—three (and its multiples). Ódhinn is again and again represented in triads of aspects, for example, Ódhinn-Vili-Vé, Ódhinn-Hœnir-Lódhurr, Ódhinn-Hœnir-Loki, and Hárr (the High)–Jafnhárr (the Equally High)–Thridhi (the Third). The oldest formulation of this type is certainly Ódhinn-Vili-Vé, which dates from the common Germanic period. We can know this because it was originally an alliterative formula. The Germanic forms of the names would have been *Wōdhanaz, Wiljōn,* and *Wīhaz.* An examination of the deeper levels of the formula will yield much of the hidden structure of Ódhinn (see table 13.2)

Wōdhanaz should be clear enough by now as that which integrates the many into a conscious whole and describes this entire process (hence, this is the most common name for the god). *Wiljōn* is the will that charges the process with a joyful dynamism. The idea of joy is expressed by this root in most of the ancient Germanic dialects, including Old English. This is the

Table 13.2. The Structure of the Odhinic Triad

Name	Meaning	Essence	Function
Wōdhanaz	inspiration	wholeness	integrative
Wiljōn	desire/joy/will	dynamism	transformational
Wīhaz	sacrality	separation	separative

power of conscious willed direction. *Wīhaz* contains a root concept of separateness, "other-ness," which is absolutely essential to the threefold working of the god as it works in all of the worlds. This is bound up with the dichotomy of the "holy" as expressed in Indo-European thought. *Wīh-* is that terrifying and mysterious aspect (the *numinosum* or *mysterium tremendum*)—the doorway between the worlds through which all who would transform themselves, gods or men, must pass. When seen from the outside, *wīhaz* can be terrifying, but once the runester becomes *wīhaz*, he sees for the first time and is therefore often feared, resented, or even hated.

Therefore, the whole describes an eternal process of evolution, of transformation—the power to shape and reshape. This process is the interplay between the two halves of the whole; and Ódhinn is the embodiment and eventual conscious model of the oscillation between the fields of light and dark through a continuous process of separation from one field, merger with the other, there to undergo transformation, followed by reintegration with the first field. Thus, the fields of darkness are sown with the seeds of light, and the fields of light are sown with the seeds of darkness. All polar fields contain the seeds of their opposites.

All of this is done by means of a will, or consciousness, that is fundamentally separate from the process itself. This is most evident in the Yggdrasill initiation, where Ódhinn binds together the realms of light and dark, life and death, conscious and unconscious. But he is not consumed by the process—*he makes use of it.* The other sources of Ódhinic wisdom also have elements of this binding of polar opposites and ultimate utilization of them by the magical Self.

For the modern runester this has many lessons to teach. The true essence of the lore is by its very nature impossible to express fully in "words," that is, in common natural language. But what can be said is that

Ódhinn's being teaches the way of the "whole-I," the "all-self," *as well as* the "higher self." This higher self is a supraconscious entity, the "holy self" or the magical ego of the runemaster. It can mingle with the natural, organic cosmos. It can mingle with the non-natural, numinous realms. It does so, however, in order that it may further its willed aims. It is the essence of the way of the true seeker, never resting, always searching in darkness and in light, high and low, in life and in death. But the process of synthesizing the polar fields is not one of neutralization but of maximization—a boring directly through to the kernel essences. Only in this way can the whole of the power be known and used.

The runes play a central role in all of these Ódhinic mysteries. It is through them that Ódhinn comprehends these processes, through them that he formulates them so that he can master and eventually (in part) manipulate them, and through this formulation that he can communicate the mysteries to his human kith and kin.

The "cosmic runes" (ON *ginnrúnar*) are innate and eternal patterns in the substance of the multiverse, indestructible and ever-growing along eternal patterns. They cannot be fully comprehended, however, because when a part of them is comprehended (internalized by a conscious being), they at once grow beyond that comprehension; this process is also eternal. Ódhinn, like the modern theoretical physicists who have followed him, knows this well and knows that his search for totality is a never-ending one. Yet he continues in his heroic struggle, as must his fellows. Those who find this prospect disheartening are not meant for the Odian path.

When Ódhinn undertook the Yggdrasill working, the primal heroic deed of consciousness was completed. The very basic and elemental systematic structure of the whole was at once won and comprehended. These runes, divided into bright runes (ON *heidhrúnar*) and murk runes (ON *myrkrúnar*), now provide the road map for the unending exploration of the multiverse. The runes held by Ódhinn may be won by humanity through following Ódhinn's example and by assimilating, as he did, the patterns of his consciousness imprinted with the runic system. (The Odian does not seek "union" with Ódhinn but seeks union only with that with which Ódhinn sought union—the Self.)

These runes represent totality in its simplest yet most whole form comprehensible to the human psychophysical complex. But as Ódhinn can never comprehend all of the cosmic runes, so humans can rarely fully comprehend all of the divine runes. However, because we are the children of the All-Father (i.e., conscious beings) and have received his primal (and only "free") gifts of consciousness (see chapter 10) we are able to ride the runeroads with the Æsir. The runes are the road map by which man can find selfhood and the gods, and in turn they provide the way through which Ódhinn can chart the edges of unknown time and space.

It should now be evident why Ódhinn is the hidden god. As popularly understood, the formulation "hidden god" indicates that unknown and unknowable "god beyond duality." No other archetype working in the realm of consciousness so perfectly represents the path to that state. The processes outlined above show how this god works; essentially, its function cannot be understood in the intellectual sense. It can be understood only through experience in magical workings of the "Ódhinic paradox." Even when this comprehension takes place, and you begin to open the runic secrets, Ódhinn will still remain a hidden god, for in actual experience the intellect and the words of human speech fail because they are phenomena of only half of the whole to which the experience belongs.

Appendix I
Runic Tables

Table 1. The Elder Futhark

Number	Shape	Major Variant Shapes	Phonetic Value(s)
1	ᚠ	ᚠ	f
2	ᚢ	ᚢ ᚢ ᚢ	u
3	ᚦ	ᚦ ᚦ	th
4	ᚨ	ᚨ ᚨ	a
5	ᚱ	ᚱ ᚱ ᚱ	r
6	ᚲ	ᛦ ᛉ ᛣ	k
7	ᚷ		g
8	ᚹ	ᚹ	w
9	ᚺ	ᚾ ᚻ	h
10	ᚾ	ᚾ ᚿ	n
11	ᛁ		i
12	ᛃ	ᛃ ᛃ ᛃ ᛡ ᛃ	j
13	ᛇ	ᛇ	i/ei
14	ᛈ	ᛈ ᛈ	p
15	ᛉ	ᛉ ᛡ ᛦ	-z ~ -R
16	ᛊ	ᛋ ᛊ ᛊ	s
17	ᛏ	ᛏ	t
18	ᛒ	ᛒ ᛒ	b
19	ᛖ	ᛖ	e
20	ᛗ		m
21	ᛚ	ᛚ	l
22	ᛜ	ᛜ ᛜ ᛝ	-ng
23	ᛞ	ᛞ	d/dh
24	ᛟ		o

Table 1. The Elder Futhark (Cont.)

No.	Name	Translation of the Name
1	*fehu*	cattle, livestock money (gold)
2	*uruz*	aurochs
3	*thurisaz*	thurs (the strong one)
4	*ansuz*	the Ase, sovereign ancestral god
5	*raidho*	wagon, chariot
6	*kenaz/kaunaz*	torch/sore
7	*gebo*	gift
8	*wunjo*	joy, pleasure
9	*hagalaz*	hail (stone)
10	*nauthiz*	need
11	*isa*	ice
12	*jera*	year (good harvest)
13	*i (h)waz*	yew
14	*perthro*	lot cup
15	*elhaz/algiz*	elk/protection
16	*sowilo*	sun
17	*tiwaz*	Týr, the sky god
18	*berkano*	birch(-goddess)
19	*ehwaz/ehwo*	horse/two horses
20	*mannaz*	man (human being)
21	*laguz/laukaz*	water/leek
22	*ingwaz*	Ing, the earth god
23	*dagaz*	day
24	*othala*	ancestral property

Table 1. The Elder Futhark (Cont.)

No.	Esoteric Interpretation of Name
1	dynamic power
2	primal, formative and fertilizing essence
3	the breaker of resistance (Thórr)
4	sovereign ancestral force (Ódhinn)
5	vehicle of path of cosmic power
6	controlled energy
7	exchanged force
8	harmony of like forces
9	seed form and primal union
10	need-fire (resistance/deliverance)
11	contraction (matter/antimatter)
12	orbit (life cycle)
13	axis (tree of life/death)
14	evolutionary force
15	protective and tutelary numen
16	sun-wheel (crystallized light)
17	sovereign order (Týr)
18	birch numen (retainer/releaser)
19	twin equine gods (trust)
20	human order from divine ancestry
21	life energy and organic growth
22	gestation-container (Yngvi)
23	twilight/dawn (paradox)
24	self-contained hereditary power

Table 2. The Anglo-Frisian Futhorc

No.	Shape	Thames Sax	Major Variants	Frisian
1	ᚹ	ᚠ	ᚹ	ᚠ ᚤ
2	ᚢ	ᚢ	ᚢ	ᚢ
3	ᚦ	ᚦ	ᚦ	ᚦ
4	ᚨ	ᚨ	ᚨ	ᚨ
5	ᚱ	ᚱ	ᚱ	ᚱ ᚾ
6	ᚺ	ᚺ	ᚴ	ᚺ
7	ᚷ	ᚷ		ᚷ
8	ᚹ	ᚹ	ᚹ	ᚹ
9	ᚻ	ᚾ	ᚻ ᛁ ᚾ	ᚾ
10	ᛏ	ᛏ	ᛠ ᛡ	ᛏ
11	ᛁ	ᛁ		ᛁ ᚤ
12	ᛜ	ᛐ	ᛐ ᛰ	ᛜ
13		ᛚ	ᛉ	ᛁ
14	ᛣ	ᛣ	ᚻ	ᛖ
15	ᛦ	ᛦ	ᛦ	ᛦ
16	ᛐ	ᛖ	ᛐ ᛐ ᛐ	ᛐ
17	↑	↑		↑
18	ᛒ	ᛒ	B	ᛒ
19	ᛗ	ᛗ		ᛗ ᛩ
20	ᛘ	ᛘ	ᛟ	ᛘ ᛩ
21	ᚱ	ᚱ		ᚱ ᚲ
22	ᚷ	ᚷ	ᚷ	ᚷ
23	ᛟ	ᛟ	ᛟ	ᛟ
24	ᛜ	ᛜ	ᛜ	ᛜ
25	ᚡ	ᚡ		ᚡ
26	ᚦ	ᚦ		
27	ᚹ	ᚹ	ᚻ ᚢ	ᚡᚥ
28	ᛘ	ᛘ	ᛘ	ᚱ
29	ᛪ		ᛪ	ᚢ
30	ᛣ		ᛣ	ᛘ
31	ᛙ		ᛙ ᛚ ᛙ	
32	ᛩ			
33	ᛯ			

Table 2. The Anglo-Frisian Futhorc (Cont.)

No.	Phonetic Values	Old English Name	Translation of Name
1	f	feoh	cattle, wealth
2	u	ūr	wild ox
3	th/dh	thorn	thorn
4	o	ōs	a god (or mouth)
5	r	rād	(a) ride
6	c/ch	cēn	torch
7	g [j/zh]	gyfu	gift
8	w	wynn	joy
9	h	haegl	hail
10	n	nȳd	need, distress
11	i	īs	ice
12	y	gēr	year
13	eo	ēoh	yew
14	p	peordh	dice box
15	x	eolhx	elks/sedge reed
16	s	sigel	sun
17	t	tīr	Tiw/sign or glory
18	b	beorc	birch/polar
19	e	eh	horse
20	m	monn	man (human being)
21	l	lagu	sea
22	ng	ing	the god Ing
23	d	dæg	day
24	e [ay] œ	ēthel	ancestral property
25	a	āc	oak
26	ae	æsc	ash
27	y	ȳr	gold decoration/bow
28	ea	ēar	earth-grave
29	eo/io	ior	serpent
30	q	(c)weordh	fire-twirl
31	k	calc	chalk/chalice
32	st	stān	stone
33	g	gār	spear

Table 3. The Younger Futhark

Number	Shape	Gørlev	Major Variants	Phonetic Value
1	ᚠ	ᚠ	ᛂ	f
2	ᚢ	ᚢ		u/o/ö/v
3	ᚦ	ᚦ	D	th/dh
4	ᚬ	ᚬ	ᚭ ᚮ	ą
5	ᚱ	ᚱ	ᚱ ᚱ	r
6	ᚴ	ᚴ	ᛘ ᛍ ⊥	k/g/ng
7	ᚼ	ᚼ	ᚽ ᛂ	h
8	ᚾ	ᚾ	ᚿ	n
9	ᛁ	ᛁ		i/e
10	ᛅ	ᛅ	ᛆ ᚼ	a
11	ᛋ	ᛋ	ᛋ ᛌ	s
12	ᛏ	ᛏ	ᛐ	t/d/nd
13	ᛒ	ᛒ	ᛓ ᛒ	b/p/mb
14	ᛘ	ᛘ	ᛘ ᛘ ᛙ ᛙ	m
15	ᛚ	ᛚ		l
16	ᛦ	ᛦ	ı	-R

Table 3. The Younger Futhark (Cont.)

No.	Old Norse Name	Translation of Name
1	*fé*	cattle, money, gold
2	*úr(r)*	drizzling rain/slag/aurochs
3	*thurs*	thurs ("giant")
4	*áss*	(the) god (= Ódhinn)
5	*reidh*	a ride, riding/vehicle/thunderclap
6	*kaun*	a sore
7	*hagall*	hail (a special rune name)
8	*naudh(r)*	need, bondage, fetters
9	*íss*	ice
10	*ár*	(good) year, harvest
11	*sól*	sun
12	*Týr*	the god Týr
13	*bjarkan*	birch(-goddess) (a special rune name)
14	*madhr*	man, human
15	*lögr*	sea, waterfall (liquid)
16	*ýr*	yew, bow of yew wood

Table 3. The Younger Futhark (Cont.)

No.	Esoteric Interpretation of Name
1	dynamic power
2	fertilizing essence
3	breaker of resistance
4	power of the word, sovereign force
5	spiritual path or journey
6	internal, magical fire or projection
7	ice seed form
8	need-fire, slavery/freedom
9	contraction *prima materia*
10	blooming forth into manifestation
11	sun-wheel/crystallized light
12	sovereign heavenly order
13	gestation/birth, instrument of the birch numen
14	human order of divine ancestry, power to connect realms
15	life energy and organic growth
16	telluric power

Table 4. The Armanen Futhork

No.	Shape	Name	Meaning
1	⚡	*fa*	Primal fire, change, reshaping, banishing of distress, sending generative principle, primal spirit
2	ᚢ	*ur*	Eternity, consistency, physicians' rune, luck, telluric magnetism, primal soul
3	ᚦ	*thorn*	Action, will to action, evolutionary power, goal setting, rune of Od-magnetic transference
4	ᚨ	*os*	Breath, spiritual well-being, word, radiating od-magnetic power
5	ᚱ	*rit*	Primal law, rightness, advice, rescue, rhythm
6	ᚲ	*ka*	Generation, power, art, ability, propagation
7	ᚺ	*hagal*	All-enclosure, spiritual leadership, protectiveness, harmony
8	ᚾ	*not*	The unavoidable, "karma," compulsion of fate
9	ᛁ	*is*	Ego, will, activity, personal power, banishing, consciousness of spiritual power, control of self and others
10	ᛃ	*ar*	Sun, wisdom, beauty, virtue, fame, well-being, protection from specters, leadership
11	ᛋ	*sig*	Solar power, victory, success, knowledge, realization, power to actualize
12	ᛏ	*tyr*	Power, success, wisdom, generation, awakening, rebirth in the spirit
13	ᛒ	*bar*	Becoming, birth, concealment, song
14	ᛚ	*laf*	Primal law, life, experience of life, love, primal water, water and ocean rune

Table 4. The Armanen Futhork (Cont.)

No	Shape	Name	Meaning
15	Ψ	*man*	Man-rune, increase, fullness, health, magic, spirit, god-man, the masculine principle in the cosmos, day-consciousness
16	⋏	*yr*	Woman-rune, instinct, greed, passion, matter, delusion, confusion, death, destruction, the negative feminine principle in the cosmos, night consciousness
17	⋌	*eh*	Marriage, lasting love, law, justice, hope, duration, rune of troth and of the dual (twin) souls
18	⋈	*gibor*	God-rune, god-all, cosmic consciousness, wedding together of powers, the generative and receptive, sacred marriage, giver and the gift, fulfillment

Appendix II
Pronunciation of Old Norse

The phonetic values provided below are those of reconstructed Old Norse (as it would have been spoken in the Viking Age). The consonants *b, d, f, l, m, t,* and *v* are just as in modern English.

a   as in "artistic"
á   as in "father"
e   as in "men"
é   as in *ay* in "bay"
i   as in it"
í   as *ee* in "feet"
o   as in "omit"
ó   as in "ore"
ö   as in "not"
ø   pronounced same as ö
u   as in "put"
ú   as in "rule"
æ   as *ai* in "hair"
œ   as *u* in "slur"
y   as *u* in German *Hütte* (*i* with rounded lips)
ý   as *u* in German *Tür* (*ee* with rounded lips)
au as *ou* in "house"
ei as *ay* in "May," *or* as *i* in "mine"
ey pronounced same as *ei*
g   always hard as in "go"
ng as in "long"
h   same as English, except before consonants, then as *wh* in "where"
j   always as *y* in "year"
p   as in English, except before *t*, then this *pt* cluster is pronounced *ft*
r   trilled *r*
s   always voiceless as in "sing"
th voiceless *th* as in "thin"
dh voiced *th* as in "the"
rl pronounced *dl*
rn pronounced *dn*
nn pronounced *dn* after long vowels and diphthongs

Glossary

Æsir: sg., Áss; genitive pl., Ása (used as a prefix to denote that the god or goddess is "of the Æsir"). ON. Race of gods corresponding to the functions of magic, law, and war.

ætt: pl., *ættir*. ON. Family or genus, used both as a name for the threefold divisions of the futhark and the eight divisions of the heavens. Also means a group or division of *eight*.

airt: Scots dialect word. See *ætt*.

bind rune: Two or more runestaves superimposed on one another, sometimes used to form *galdrastafir*.

Edda: ON. Word of uncertain origin, used as the title of ancient manuscripts dealing with mythology. The *Elder* or *Poetic Edda* is a collection of poems composed between 800 and 1270 C.E.; the *Younger* or *Prose Edda* was written by Snorri Sturluson in 1222 C.E. as a codification of the mythology of Ásatrú for the skalds.

erilaz: pl., *eriloz*. See Erulian.

Erulian: Member of the ancient gild of runesmasters who formed an intertribal network of initiates in the Germanic mysteries.

etin: Developed from OE *eoten* and ON *jötunn*. A type of "giant" known for its strength. Also a generic name for "giant" (in ON Jötunheimr, etc.).

etin-wife: A female etin taken in magical marriage.

fetch: See *fylgja*.

fetch-wife: The fetch in female form. See also *valkyrja*.

formáli: pl., *formálar*. ON. Formulaic speeches used to load action with magical intent.

fylgja: pl., *fylgjur*. ON A numinous being attached to every individual, which is the repository of all past action and which accordingly affects the person's life; the personal divinity. Visualized as a contrasexual entity, an animal, or an abstract shape.

galdr: pl., *galdrar*. ON. Originally "incantation" (the verb *gala* is used also for "to crow"); later meant magic in general but especially verbal magic.

galdrastafr: pl., *galdrastafir*. ON. Literally "stave of incantations." A magic sign of various types, made up of bind runes and/or pictographs and/or ideographs.

Germanic: (1) The proto-language spoken by the Germanic peoples before the various dialects (e.g., English, German, Gothic, Scandinavian) developed; also a collective term for the languages belonging to this group. (2) A collective term for all peoples descended from the Germanic-speaking group (e.g., the English, the Germans, the Scandinavians). Norse or Nordic is a subgroup of Germanic and refers only to the Scandinavian branch of the Germanic heritage.

Gothic: Designation of a now extinct Germanic language and people who spoke it. Last speakers known in the Crimean in the eighteenth century.

hamingja: pl., *hamingjur*. ON. Mobile magical force rather like the *mana* and *manitu* of other traditions. Often defined as "luck," "shape-shifting power," and "guardian spirit."

hamr: ON. The plastic image-forming substance that surrounds each individual, making the physical form. It may be collected and reformed by magical power (*hamingja*) according to will (*hugr*).

hugr: ON. A portion of the psychophysical complex corresponding to the conscious mind and the faculty of cognition.

metagenetics: Concept of characteristics of structures, that might at first seem to be "spiritual," inherited along genetic lines. Term made current by Stephen A. McNallen.

minni: ON. The faculty of "memory"; the images stored in the deep mind from aeons past.

multiverse: A term descriptive of the *many* states of being (worlds) that constitute the "universe."

niding: Developed from ON *nídh* (insult) and *nídhingr* (a vile wretch). Used in the context of cursing by the use of satirical or insulting poetry.

Norn: pl., Nornir (or English Norns). ON. One of the three complex cosmic beings in female form that embody the mechanical process of cause and effect and serve as a matrix for evolutionary force.

numen: adj., numinous. Living, nonphysical, or magical aspects within the cosmic order, not necessarily meant in the animistic sense; that which partakes of spiritual power.

Odian: A technical term for the "theology" of the Erulian. Distinguished from the Odinist by the fact that the Odian does not *worship* Ódhinn but seeks to emulate his pattern of self-transformation.

Old English: The language spoken by the Anglo-Saxon tribes in southern Britain from about 450 to 1100 c.e. Also known as Anglo-Saxon.

Old Norse: The language spoken by West Scandinavians (in Norway, Iceland, and parts of Britain) in the Viking Age (ca. 800–1100 c.e.). Also language of the *Eddas* and of skaldic poetry.

runecraft: The use of rune skill (esoteric knowledge) for causing changes in the objective environment.

runelore: A general term for esoteric teachings.

rune skill: Intellectual knowledge of runelore.

runestave: The physical shape of a runic character.

runester: From ON *rýnstr*, "one most skilled in runes." General term for one involved in deep-level rune skill.

rune wisdom: Ability to apply rune skill to deep-level visions of the world and its workings; runic philosophy.

runework: The use of rune skill for causing changes or development in the subjective universe; self-developmental work.

skald: ON term for a poet who composes highly formal, originally magical verse.

skaldcraft: The magical force of poetry; verbal magic (*galdr*). Also, the "science" of folk etymology in which magical, suprarational associations are made between words based on sounds.

tally lore: Esoteric study of number symbolism.

thurs: From ON *thurs*. A giant characterized by great strength and age, for example, the rime-thurses or frost-giants.

valkyrja: pl., *valkyrjur*. ON. "Chooser of the Fallen" (i.e., the slain). Protective *valkyrja*-like numinous qualities that become attached to certain persons who attract them; a linking force between men and gods (especially Ódhinn).

Vanir: sg., Van. ON. The race of gods corresponding to the fertility, prosperity, eroticism functions.

World: (1) The entire cosmos or universe. (2) One of the nine levels of being or planes of existence that make up the ordered cosmos.

Yggdrasill: ON. The cosmic tree of nine worlds or planes of the multiverse.

Bibliography

Arntz, Helmut. *Handbuch der Runenkunde.* Halle/Saale: Niemeyer, 1935, 1944.

Balzli, Johannes. *Guido von List: Der Wiederentdecker uralter arischer Weischeit.* Vienna: Guido-von-List-Gesellschaft, 1917.

Baum, Paul F., trans., ed. *Anglo-Saxon Riddles of the Exeter Book.* Durham, NC: Duke University Press, 1963.

Blachetta, Walther. *Das Buch der deutschen Sinnzeichen.* Berlin-Lichterfelde: Widukind/Boss, 1941.

Bugge, Sophus. *Norges Indskrifter med de ældre Runer.* Christiana: Brogger, 1905–1913.

Caesar, Julius. *The Conquest of Gaul.* Translated by S. A. Handford. Harmondsworth, UK: Penguin, 1951.

Ellis, Hilda R. *The Road to Hel.* Cambridge: Cambridge University Press, 1943.

Ellis Davidson, Hilda R. *Gods and Myths of Northern Europe.* Harmondsworth, UK: Penguin, 1964.

Derolez, René. *Runica Manuscripta.* Brugge: Rijks-Universiteit te Ghent, 1954.

Dickens, Bruce. *Runic and Heroic Poems of the Old Teutonic Peoples.* Cambridge: Cambridge University Press, 1915.

Dumézil, Georges. *Gods of the Ancient Northmen.* Edited by E. Haugen. Berkeley, CA: University of California Press, 1973.

Düwel, Klaus. *Runenkunde.* Sammlung Metzler 72. Stuttgart: J. B. Metzler, 1968, 1983.

Eckhardt, Karl August. *Irdische Unsterblichkeit: Germanischer Glaube an die Wiederverkörperung in der Sippe.* Weimar: Bohlau, 1937.

Eliade, Mircea. *The Myth of the Eternal Return or, Cosmos and History.* Translated by W. R. Trask. Bollingen Series 46. Princeton, NJ: Princeton University Press, 1971.

_____.*Shamanism: Archaic Techniques of Ecstasy.* Translated by W. R. Trask. Bollingen Series 76. Princeton, NJ: Princeton University Press, 1971.

Elliott, Ralph. *Runes, an Introduction.* Manchester: Manchester University Press, 1959.

Fox, Denton, and Hermann Pálsson, trans. *Grettir's Saga.* Toronto: University of Toronto Press, 1974.

Gorsleben, Rudolf John. *Die Hoch-Zeit der Menschheit.* Leipzig: Koehler & Amelang, 1930.

216 / BIBLIOGRAPHY

Grimm, Jacob. *Teutonic Mythology.* Translated by S. Stallybrass. 4 vols.
New York: Dover, 1966.

Grönbech, Vilhelm. *The Culture of the Teutons.* London: Oxford University
Press, 1931.

Hartmann, Franz. "Review: Guido von List. Die Bilderschrift der Ario-
Germanen: Ario-Germanische Hieroglyphik." *Neue Lotusblüten*
Jahrgang 1910, pp. 370–71.

Hauck, Karl. *Goldbrakteaten aus Sievern.* Munich: Fink, 1970.

Hollander, Lee M., trans. *The Poetic Edda.* Austin, TX: University of
Texas Press, 1962.

Jones, Gwyn, trans. *The Vatndalers' Saga.* Princeton, NJ: Princeton University Press, 1944.

Jung, C. G. "Wotan" in Collected Works, vol. 10. Translated by R. F. C.
Hull. Princeton, NJ: Princeton University Press, pp. 179–193.

Kershaw, Nora, ed., trans. *Stories and Ballads of the Far Past.* Cambridge:
Cambridge University Press, 1921. (*Sörlatháttr*, pp. 43–57.)

Krause, Wolfgang. *Was man in Runen ritzte.* Halle/Salle: Niemeyer, 1935.

_____. *Runeninschriften im älteren Futhark* Halle/Saale: Niemeyer,
1937.

_____. *Runeninscriften im älteren Futhark.* 2 vols. Göttingen: Vande-
hoeck & Ruprecht, 1966.

Kummer, Siegfried Adolf. *Die heilige Runenmacht.* Hamburg: Uranus-
Verlag, 1932.

_____. *Runen-Magie.* Dresden: Gartmann, 1934/35.

List, Guido von. *Das Geheimnis der Runen.* Vienna: Guido-von-List-
Gesellschaft, 1912.

_____. *Die Religion der Ario-Germanen in ihrer Esoterik und Exoterik.*
Berlin-Lichterfelde: Guido-von-List Verlag, 1910.

Marby, Friedrich Bernhard. *Marby-Runen-Bücherei.* 4 vols. Stuttgart:
Marby-Verlag, 1931–1935.

Marstrander, C. J. S. "Om runene og runenavenes oprindelse." *Nordisk
Tidskrift for Sprogvidenskab,* 1 (1928), pp. 1–67.

Mayer, R. M. "Runenstudien." *Beiträge zur Geschichte der deutschen
Sprache und Literatur,* 21 (1896), pp. 162–184.

Moltke, Erik. *Runerne i Danmark og Deres Oprindelse.* Copenhagen:
Forum, 1976.

Morris, William, and Eiríkur Magnusson, trans., ed. *The Völsunga Saga.*
New York: Collier Books, 1962.

Much, Rudolf. *Die Germania des Tacitus.* 3rd ed. Heidelberg: Carl Winter,
1967.

Neckel, Gustav (ed). *Edda: Die Lieder des Codex Regius nebst verwandten Denkmälern*. Heidelberg: Carl Winter, 1962.

Page, R. I. *An Introduction to English Runes*. London: Methuen, 1973.

Pálsson, Hermann, and Paul Edwards, trans. *Egil's Saga*. Middlesex, UK: Penguin, 1976.

Saxo Grammaticus. *The History of the Danes*, vol 1, translated and edited by Peter Fisher and H. R. Ellis Davidson. Suffolk, UK: Boydell & Brewer, 1979.

Schneider, Karl. *Die germanischen Runennamen*. Meisenheim: Anton Hain, 1956.

Spiesberger, Karl. *Runenexerzietien für Jedermann*. Freiburg: Bauer, 1976.

_____. *Runenmagie*. Berlin: R. Schikowski, 1955.

Sturluson, Snorri. *The Prose Edda*. Translated by A. G. Brodeur. New York: American Scandinavian Foundation, 1929.

_____. *Heimskringla*. Translated by Lee M. Hollander. Austin: University of Texas Press, 1962.

Tacitus, Cornelius. *The Agricola and the Germania*. Translated by H. Mattingly. Middlesex, UK: Penguin, 1970.

Thorsson, Edred. *Futhark: A Handbook of Rune Magic*. York Beach, ME: Samuel Weiser, 1984.

_____. trans., ed. *The Icelandic Galdrabók: A 16th Century Grimoire*. Austin: The Rune-Gild, 1985.

Tolkien, Chistopher, trans., ed. *Hervarar saga ok Heidhreks konungs: The Sage of King Heidrek the Wise*. London: Thomas Nelson & Sons, 1960.

Tupper, Frederick (ed). *The Riddles of the Exeter Book*. Boston: Ginn, 1910.

Turville-Petre, E. O. G. *Myth and Religion of the North*. New York: Holt, Rinehart and Winston, 1964.

Vries, Jan de. *Altgermanishe Religionsgeschichte*. 2 vols. Berlin: de. Gruyter, 1956–1957.

Wimmer, L. F. A. *Die Runenschrift*. Berlin: Weidemann, 1887.

Index

About the Author

Edred Thorsson received his doctorate in Germanic Languages and Medieval Studies from the University of Texas. He translated Guido von List's *The Secret of Runes*, taught humanities at the university level, and founded Runa-Raen Press. He is the author of *Futhark: A Handbook of Rune Magic* and *Runecaster's Handbook*. He lives in Austin, Texas where he practices rune magic.